The Battle of the Somme: The History and Legacy Battle

By Charles River Editors

A picture of British soldiers marching to the front

About Charles River Editors

Charles River Editors is a boutique digital publishing company, specializing in bringing history back to life with educational and engaging books on a wide range of topics. Keep up to date with our new and free offerings with this 5 second sign up on our weekly mailing list, and visit Our Kindle Author Page to see other recently published Kindle titles.

We make these books for you and always want to know our readers' opinions, so we encourage you to leave reviews and look forward to publishing new and exciting titles each week.

Introduction

A picture of British soldiers advancing in September 1916

The Battle of the Somme

"Somme. The whole history of the world cannot contain a more ghastly word." - Friedrich Steinbrecher, a German officer.

World War I, also known in its time as the "Great War" or the "War to End all Wars", was an unprecedented holocaust in terms of its sheer scale. Fought by men who hailed from all corners of the globe, it saw millions of soldiers do battle in brutal assaults of attrition which dragged on for months with little to no respite. Tens of millions of artillery shells and untold hundreds of millions of rifle and machine gun bullets were fired in a conflict that demonstrated man's capacity to kill each other on a heretofore unprecedented scale, and as always, such a war brought about technological innovation at a rate that made the boom of the Industrial Revolution seem stagnant.

The enduring image of World War I is of men stuck in muddy trenches, and of vast armies deadlocked in a fight neither could win. It was a war of barbed wire, poison gas, and horrific losses as officers led their troops on mass charges across No Man's Land and into a hail of bullets. While these impressions are all too true, they hide the fact that trench warfare was dynamic and constantly evolving throughout the war as all armies struggled to find a way to break through the opposing lines.

Though World War I is almost synonymous with trench warfare, that method of combat was nothing new. There had been extensive use of trenches during the later stages of the American Civil War (1864-1865), and trench warfare was constant during the Second Boer War (1899-1902), the Russo-Japanese War (1904-1905), and the Balkan Wars (1912-1913). These conflicts showed that modern firepower combined with entrenched positions gave a decisive advantage to the defender, yet European observers failed to learn any lessons from these conflicts, and the scale of trench warfare in World War I far eclipsed anything seen before or since, especially on the Western Front.

Since the Industrial Revolution, arms and materiel output had increased by orders of magnitude, as had the quality and uniformity of the products. Several developments had already taken place in the years building up to the conflict, stepping stones towards the vast escalation in military innovation which took place immediately prior to and during World War I. Chief among these was the invention of smokeless gunpowder, which took place concurrently among several powers between 1890 and 1905. This was a crucial development, as it eliminated the literal "fog of war" which in vast quantities obscured the battlefield entirely and on an individual level both gave away the position of marksmen and made it impossible for them to fire accurately unless they moved away from their own smoke-cloud. Further innovations included the adoption into service of the first belt-fed machine guns, predecessors of those which would wreak such slaughter in the trenches, and the development of cannon which did not roll backwards after each shot as 19th century pieces did, but remained fixed in place.

The arms race before the war and the attempt to break the deadlock of the Western and Eastern Fronts by any means possible changed the face of battle in ways that would have previously been deemed unthinkable. Before 1914, flying machines were objects of public curiosity; the first flights of any account on rotor aircraft had been made less than 5 years before and were considered to be the province of daredevils and lunatics. By 1918, all the great powers were fielding squadrons of fighting aircraft armed with machine guns and bombs, to say nothing of light reconnaissance planes. Tanks, a common feature on the battlefield by 1918, had not previously existed outside of the realm of science fiction stories written by authors like H.G. Wells. Machine guns had gone from being heavy, cumbersome pieces with elaborate water-cooling systems to single-man-portable, magazine-fed affairs like the Chauchat, the Lewis Gun and the M1918 BAR. To these grim innovations were added flamethrowers, hand grenades, zeppelins, observation balloons, poison gas, and other improvements or inventions that revolutionized the face of warfare.

These technological developments led to an imbalance. Before the introduction of the man-portable light machine gun (which took place in the second half of the war), not to mention tanks (which also joined the fight late in the game), defensive firepower vastly outweighed offensive capability. Massed batteries of artillery, emplaced heavy machine guns, barbed wire entanglements, and bewildering fortifications meant that ground could not be taken except at incredible cost. This led to the (somewhat unjustified) criticism famously leveled at the generals of World War I that their soldiers were "lions led by donkeys". Certainly, every army that fought in the Great War had its share of officers, at all levels of command, who were incompetent, unsuitable, foolish, or just plain stupid, but there were plenty of seasoned professionals who understood their job and did it well. The main problem facing commanders in the war was that there was such a bewildering array of new armaments, with such vast destructive potential, that previous military doctrines were virtually useless. Cavalry, which had been expected to play a major role both as reconnaissance and as "mounted infantry", operating in much the same way as airborne and mechanized troops would later to rapidly outflank enemy positions, quickly proved useless. Frontal infantry assaults were cut to shreds by enemy defensive fire, but there seemed to be no major alternative. Ground had to be taken, even if at great cost, and to do so, more destructive weapons were devised, tested and deployed.

Needless to say, the First World War came at an unfortunate time for those who would fight in it. After an initial period of relatively rapid maneuver during which the German forces pushing through Belgium and the French and British forces attempting to stymie them made an endless series of abortive flanking movements that extended the lines to the sea, a stalemate naturally tended to develop. The infamous trench lines soon snaked across the French and Belgian countryside, creating an essentially futile static slaughterhouse whose sinister memory remains to this day.

The Battle of the Somme is still controversial for the British to this day. On July 1, 1916, the first day of fighting, more British soldiers were killed or wounded than at any time before or since, including D-Day in World War II. The commander, General Douglas Haig, was revered for most of his lifetime, then dubbed the Butcher of the Somme, and now is viewed as a skilled man in a very difficult position who made a number of avoidable mistakes. British schoolchildren are still taught about the devastating battle, which saw over 3 million soldiers participate and over 1 million killed, wounded, or captured, and its effects on the rest of the war.

The Battle of the Somme: The History and Legacy of World War I's Biggest Battle analyzes one of the Great War's most important conflicts, and how it was emblematic of the stalemate that came from new technology and trench warfare. Along with pictures of important people, places, and events, you will learn about the Battle of the Somme like never before.

The Start of the War

By the 20th century, warfare was nothing new to the European powers, especially when it came to fighting each other. Conflicts had been a mainstay on the European continent for over two millennia. Even after the Napoleonic wars had enveloped Europe in large scale war for nearly 20 years in the 19th century, the Europeans' imperialism continued unabated. It would take the devastation of World War I to shock Europe and jolt the world's superpowers out of their imperialistic tendencies.

After Napoleon and the French were was finally defeated in 1815 by a coalition of European nations, Europe went about their most serious attempt to create peace on the continent. Even before the fighting had ended, most major European powers had been meeting in Vienna and established a congress in 1814. A series of agreements were reached between the coalition and the defeated French to end the fighting.

However, the Europeans continued to conduct business as usual, spending much of the 19th century engaged in imperialism across the world. The natural response of the European nations was to establish alliances that would maintain at least a balance of power. In 1873, German chancellor Otto van Bismarck reached an alliance with Austria-Hungary's despot and the Russian czar. The French signed alliances with Britain and Russia, who had left its previous alliance over tension brought about by Austria-Hungary's intervention in the Balkans. By then, Italy had joined the German alliance.

Although a couple of wars were fought on the European continent during the 19th century, an uneasy peace was mostly maintained across the continent for most of the 19th century after Napoleon. Despite this ostensible peace, the Europeans were steadily conducting arms races against each other, particularly Germany and Britain. Britain had been the world's foremost naval power for centuries, but Germany hoped to build its way to naval supremacy. The rest of Europe joined in on the arms race in the decade before the war started.

With Europe anticipating a potential war, all that was missing was a conflagration. That would start in 1908, when Austria-Hungary annexed Bosnia-Herzegovina in the Balkan Peninsula, drawing it into dispute with Russia. Moreover, this upset neighboring Serbia, which was an independent nation. From 1912-1913, a conflict was fought in the Balkans between the Balkan League and the Ottoman Empire, resulting in the weakening of the Ottoman Turks. After the First Balkan War, a second was fought months later between members of the Balkan League itself.

The final straw came June 28, 1914, when a Serbian assassinated Archduke Franz Ferdinand, the heir to the throne of Austria-Hungary, in Sarajevo, Bosnia. The world reacted with horror to the death of Franz Ferdinand and Sophie, nowhere more so than throughout Austria-Hungary, where there was widespread rioting against innocent Serbian citizens living within the empire's borders. It is surmised that many of those displaced eventually made their way back across the border to Serbia as refugees, further inflaming sentiment against Austrians and making an already volatile situation that much worse. Expressions of horror and commiseration came in from Germany, France, Britain (although the public and the government's attention there were far more focused on the rapidly escalating crisis in Ireland, where the independence movement had turned violent), and even Austria's recent enemy, Italy. Russia also offered its condolences, which was quite hypocritical given that the Russian government was almost certainly aware of the Serbian plot.

Overwhelmingly, the Great Powers sided with Austria, and a joint Austro-Hungarian and German demand was presented to the Serbian government to commence an internal investigation into the assassination, but the Serbian Ministry of Foreign Affairs dismissed such a request out of hand, claiming that there was absolutely nothing to investigate. This further aggravated an already awkward situation.

In the wake of the investigation into the death of Franz Ferdinand and the resulting trial and sentences that followed, along with the verdict of the court inculpating Serbia for the murders, the Austro-Hungarian Empire ultimately issued a letter to Serbia which became known as the July Ultimatum. This inflammatory letter demanded that the Kingdom of Serbia repudiate in writing the acts of the terrorists intent on destabilizing the legitimacy of the Austro-Hungarian monarchy and their hold over Bosnia-Herzegovina, and it also reminded the Serbian government that it had bound itself to abide by the terms of the agreement ceding it to Austria-Hungary in the first place. The letter also listed 10 key points which Serbia was expected to accept within 48 hours, and it threatened retaliation in the case of non-compliance.

The points listed were as follows:

1. Serbia must renounce all propaganda designed to inspire hatred towards Austria-Hungary and which might prove harmful to its territorial integrity.

2. The Organization known as the People's Defence must be disbanded forthwith, along with all organizations of a similar ilk.

3. All propaganda against Austria-Hungary published in public documents, including school textbooks, is to be eliminated forthwith.

4. All officers and government officials named by the Austro-Hungarian government are to be removed from office immediately.

5. Members of the Austro-Hungarian government will be dispatched immediately to Belgrade, where they are to be given every assistance in suppressing subversive movements.

6.   All those involved in Franz Ferdinand's assassination are to be brought to trial forthwith, with the assistance of police investigators from Austria-Hungary.

7.   Major Vojislav Tankosic and Milan Ciganovic, known participants in the assassination of the royal couple, are to be immediately arrested.

8.   The Serbian government must cease all collusion in the transportation of weapons and equipment across the Austro-Hungarian Border, dismissing and disciplining the Border Patrol officials at Sabac and Loznica, who abetted the Sarajevo conspirators.

9.   Provide suitable explanation to the Austro-Hungarian government with regards to the actions undertaken by certain Serbian officials, who have demonstrated an attitude of hostility in their negotiations with the Austrian government.

10.   Immediately notify the Austro-Hungarian government once these measures have been enacted.

The letter set off a frantic flurry of activity in Serbia, but not of the kind the Austro-Hungarians wanted, aside from those in office who were clearly spoiling for a fight. Serbia telegraphed to St Petersburg asking for support, which Russia promised in the event of a fight. Reassured, Serbia then mobilized its armed forces before sending a reply to the July Ultimatum that conceded both points 8 and 10 but rejected the remaining points. The Serbs disguised their explicit refusal with a wealth of diplomatic actions that did nothing to fool the Austro-Hungarian government. The response from the empire was swift; the Austro-Hungarian ambassador in Belgrade was recalled, and troops began to prepare in for mobilization.

A propaganda cartoon after the assassination that asserted "Serbia must die!"

The day after the Austro-Hungarian ambassador departed from Belgrade, a convoy of Serbian troops being transported down the Danube River by steamer drifted off course towards the Austro-Hungarian bank near Temes-Kubin, where the local garrison commander ordered shots fired into the air to discourage them from landing. He wisely avoided firing upon the boats, which might well have precipitated a full-scale crisis, but as it was, his level-headedness would be to no avail. Unfortunately, the report which reached Emperor Franz Joseph I in Vienna about this incident inaccurately portrayed the trifling affair as a bloody last-ditch skirmish, and Franz Joseph I responded by declaring war. The Austrian Army was brought forward to a state of full mobilization, and the allotted divisions moved forward to their position on the Serbian border.

This was the move that set the dominoes of war in motion. Russia and France immediately mobilized their armies in response to the Austro-Hungarian threat, as they were required to do so according to the terms of the Secret Treaty of 1892, which stated that any mobilization of members of the Triple Alliance must be met. The initial, limited mobilization by Austria-Hungary was followed by a full-scale Russian one, which in turn was followed by a full-scale German and Austro-Hungarian call-up, which in turn precipitated a French one and finally a British one. Thus, with a suddenness that startled even those who felt it was inevitable, the major European powers all found themselves at war.

Although there had been explicit displays of commiseration and sympathy for Austria and widespread condemnation of Serbia's actions in the immediate aftermath of Franz Ferdinand's assassination, the attitude of the great powers towards Austria as the notional aggrieved party became substantially chillier as Austria insisted on virtually bullying Serbia over the whole affair. The British Prime Minister, Asquith, complained in an official letter that Serbia had no hope of appeasing Austria diplomatically, and that the terms of the July Ultimatum would've been impossible to meet even if Serbia was willing to do so. Indeed, it appears as though such an exacting document had been drafted precisely because Serbia didn't have a hope of complying, even if they had so wished, and thus Austria-Hungary would be able to go to war and punish them properly for the outrage perpetrated against their royal family.

100 years removed from the assassination, it might be unfair to say that it caused World War I, but it certainly started it. Historians still debate whether the Great War would have occurred even if Franz Ferdinand and Sophie lived out their lives in peace and comfort, but many believe that while it might've come months or years down the road, it was inevitable. The tangled web of alliances at cross-purposes, the growing diplomatic tensions, the arms race, the belligerence of newly powerful states such as Germany, the interference in other sovereign countries' affairs, and the relentless politicking all pointed towards one tragic outcome.

As for the parties themselves, it's apparent that much of the blame can be shouldered by the Serbian government. To this day, it's still unclear how much the King and Prime Minister knew about the plots and actions carried out by Dimitrijević and his associates in the Black Hand, but they were obviously privy to the official communications that involved Dimitrijević in his capacity as the head of Serbian Military Intelligence. Furthermore, it was the Serbian government, not the Black Hand (which at that point was virtually synonymous with Dimitrijević and Military Intelligence in any case) that provided Princip, Grabež, Cubrilovic, and the other conspirators with their firearms, explosives, training, and the means to cross the border into Bosnia. The People's Defence, the clandestine group within Bosnia, had been almost completely taken over by Serbian Military Intelligence and was effectively acting as a shell organization. Government officials from several different agencies had colluded with the conspirators on many occasions, with the end result that on the day of the assassination, the assassins were in place, suitably organized, well-armed for their purpose, and ready for action. At the same time, there are strong indications that several officials within the Serbian government (with or without sanction from on high) attempted to warn their Austro-Hungarian counterparts of what was to come.

Another country that must bear a share of the blame is Russia. According to the confession given by Dimitrijević at the end of his 1917 trial in Salonika, Russia was fully aware of his activities, and he had no reason to lie at that point. Indeed, according to Dimitrijević, the Russian Military Attachè in Belgrade had guaranteed that Russia would stand with Serbia against Austria-Hungary in the event that the operation was compromised, and that he had received funds from Russia to carry out the assassination. An investigative journalist attempting to uncover the truth received a fairly unconvincing testimony from the Russian Military Attachè, who denied any involvement. The Russian Military Attachè claimed that his Assistant had been in charge during the period leading up to the assassination, and that Dimitrijević never apprised him of his plans or intentions. It has also been suggested that the Tsar, or at the very least the Prime Minister, were aware of a forthcoming attempt against Franz Ferdinand's life and were not opposed to it happening. Russia had a vested interest both in weakening the Austro-Hungarian Empire and in destabilizing its hold on the Balkans as this might well potentially give it access to the strategically invaluable Mediterranean ports without having to pass through the Turkish-controlled Bosphorus and Dardanelles straits, which hampered its attempts to increase its naval power outside of the Black Sea.

Even Austria-Hungary, despite being the aggrieved party, had a hand in what followed the assassination. The Austro-Hungarian military had resisted many attempts at pacification with Serbia, including policies advocated by Franz Ferdinand himself, and it continued to pursue a policy of aggressive saber-rattling. Furthermore, the Governor of Bosnia, Oskar Potiorek, was a rigid and stubborn individual who viewed Slavic patriots as a national security threat and ruthlessly punished them accordingly, further inflaming anti-Austrian sentiment in a newly created province that required the most delicate of management rather than hamfisted pacification attempts. His refusal to countenance the use of improperly dressed troops to shield Franz Ferdinand and his halting of the motorcade in a vulnerable position near the bank of the river were symptomatic of his stubbornness, and his decision to remain idle while Sarajevo tore apart the homes of hundreds of innocent Serbs is evidence of his poor character.

Ironically, one of the few people who had no blame in what was to come was Franz Ferdinand himself. A choleric individual with the typical Austrian aristocrat's condescending attitude towards the subordinate Hungarian population, he was nonetheless no more prejudiced than many during his time and a great deal less than most; after all, he married a woman from the Czech aristocracy who was beneath his station. On top of that, his attitude towards Serbia and the Slavic issue was remarkably conciliatory for someone in his position. He went to his death unwittingly even after bravely continuing his public appearance despite having a hand grenade hurled at him. It is unfortunate for Franz Ferdinand that his birth and position made him an ideal target, but as history and fate would have it, he was simply the right man in the wrong place at the wrong time.

When World War I began in August 1914, all armies envisioned a war of movement that would lead to a quick victory. Cavalry units little changed since the Napoleonic era would act as scouts, skirmishers, and as a screen for the main army, and coming behind these would be masses of infantry with relatively few machine guns and field artillery as support. There was little in the way of aerial reconnaissance, and radio communication was in its infancy, to the extent that radio transmissions were often sent in the clear with no attempt at encryption. This was especially true of Russian communications, but all armies were guilty of this in the early days. Thus while it could be easy to find out enemy dispositions, it remained difficult to communicate this to friendly units in the field. Armies often moved blind, or with only the vaguest idea of the disposition of enemy troops.

For all sides at the start, the emphasis was on attack. Little thought was given to defensive systems except by Belgium, which was a neutral nation and relied on a massive system of forts to delay any invader long enough for guarantors such as the United Kingdom to come to its aid. As it turned out, this was exactly what happened. When Germany violated Belgian neutrality to sweep into France as part of their Schlieffen Plan, it brought the British Empire into the war on the side of the Entente with France and Russia against the Central Powers of Germany, Austro-Hungary, and the Ottoman Empire. Other countries would soon join in the fighting.

Both sides quickly realized they had miscalculated the strength of the forts. The Belgians thought they would hold out longer than they did, while the Germans thought they would fall more quickly. The Germans believed they could reduce the forts in only a couple of days, but the defenders managed to hold out for 10 days. In the end, Belgium lost 90% of its territory in the opening weeks of the war, but the German timetable for the invasion of France was thrown into disarray.

This offensive spirit was seen in other ways. Troops were not supplied with steel helmets to protect them while firing from entrenched positions, and there was a marked shortage in barbed wire, shovels, and other equipment necessary for digging in and fighting from trenches. In fact, generals emphasized the idea of constant attack so much that in some of the opening battles, French commanders ordered their men to remove the bolts from their rifles and take German positions at the point of the bayonet. This reliance on *élan* made for good newspaper headlines, but exchanging a modern army for a medieval one led to horrible casualties, and the practice was soon stopped by even the most starry-eyed commanders.

A picture of French soldiers charging with bayonets

Despite the German timetable being delayed, they still penetrated deep into French territory, and only a stubborn defense, plus the exhaustion of the German troops, kept them from taking Paris. When one of the German armies turned to flank the French defenders, it left a gap in the German line that the British Expeditionary Force and the French were quick to exploit, and in a series of engagements later dubbed the Battle of the Marne (September 5-12, 1914), Allied forces pushed forward. The Germans, exhausted and disorganized, started pulling back until they stopped at the River Aisne, a broad river with a high ridge on its far bank. From there, the German gunners set up their artillery batteries and ranged their guns while the infantry dug in on the ridge. The British attacked, and the First Battle of the Aisne (September 12-15, 1914) was the first of the war to see extensive use of trenches. When successive waves of British charges up the ridge were repulsed with heavy casualties and the German expertise at gunnery had become all too apparent, the British dug in as well. To either side of them, the French did the same, and the positions along the Aisne would be pretty much the same three years later.

The lines during the battle

When the assault across the Aisne ground to a halt, the French and British tried to outflank the Germans to the north, but they were stopped once again. Undeterred, they repeatedly tried to flank to the north in a frustrating series of battles lasting through to mid-October that has been dubbed "The Race to the Sea." In the end, the opposing armies found themselves dug in from the Swiss border to the North Sea, a distance of some 475 miles. Trench warfare had begun in earnest.

Thus, the factors determining the heavy focus of action at Ypres included both geographical and military considerations. The town of Ypres represented the westernmost Belgian town of any size and controlled a fairly important road and communications junction. It also lay in a shallow bowl formed by a series of low ridges rising some 160 feet above the surrounding flatlands at their highest point. These terrain features possessed considerable military value for the long-range observation they enabled over the countryside.

The deployment of Allied forces also had a bearing on the development of Ypres as a point of particularly bitter contests for much of the rest of the war. To the north, Belgian forces held the line to the nearby coast, and initially, the Belgian forces, led personally at times by their courageous monarch, King Albert I, attempted to counterattack the German advance. However, the Germans lured their less experienced adversaries into a trap at the village of Weerde, near Antwerp, and decimated one of their major assault columns. The American journalist Edward Alexander Powell described it vividly: "At 5:30 to the minute the whistles of the officers sounded shrilly and the mile-long line of men swept forward cheering. […] Then, Hell itself broke loose. The whole German front, which for the past several hours had replied but feebly to the Belgian fire, spat a continuous stream of lead and flame. The rolling crash of musketry and the ripping snarl of machine guns were stabbed by the vicious *pom-pom-pom-pom-pom* of the quick-firers. […] Back through the hedges, through the ditches, over the roadway came the Belgian infantry, crouching, stooping, running for their lives." (Essen, 1917, 225).

King Albert I

After this bloody reverse, the Belgians changed their strategy to stand fully on the defensive, and they even broke the coastal dikes to flood the terrain in front of their positions with the waters of the North Sea. This effectively blocked the Germans from advancing anywhere north of Ypres, though it also freed German forces for use elsewhere.

Furthermore, Ypres created a salient in the line – a projecting lobe that formed the most advanced Allied position for many years and represented the final scrap of unoccupied Belgium – made it a focus for offensives by both sides. The British Expeditionary Force (BEF) deployed precisely at the Ypres salient. Field Marshal Sir Douglas Haig and Sir John French convinced themselves that a decisive breakthrough at Ypres remained possible with just another "slight push," despite constant overwhelming proof that it was not. As a result, the British command's aggression inevitably channeled itself into these few square miles of land, and the French, whose lines stretched south from Ypres, also participated in the fighting there.

Those few miles of forward projection encouraged the fond delusions of the British leaders that it offered a jumping-off point for crashing through decisively to Antwerp and then into Germany. The Germans, on the other hand, viewed it as a location where they might hope to pierce the Allied line and break through to Calais, cutting off the BEF from reinforcement and resupply as well as forcing the surrender of the Belgians. With the British and Belgians eliminated from the continent, the Germans could then mop up the French at their leisure, or so their planners anticipated.

Each side, therefore, imagined Ypres would be the breakthrough point where they could pierce the enemy lines and bring the approaching trench-bound stalemate – a situation none of the powers had expected or wanted – to a rapid close. Thus, each party ensured that no such dramatic breakthrough could occur by concentrating their offensive forces head to head at Ypres.

The Impasse

Early fighting made clear that neither side was prepared for fighting from trenches. While all had been trained in making simple trenches as temporary defenses before continuing an advance, no military commander had envisioned the massive trench systems that would develop during the war. It was apparent something had to be done, but the high commands continued with the same mistakes, thinking that more guns and more men were all that was needed to achieve a breakthrough. As a result, lower officers and men in the ranks started devising their own tactics to kill the enemy and stay alive.

The terrain through which the front line cut was varied. Near the Flemish coast, the land was low and men digging down even two or three feet hit water. Further south in the Argonne, there was also a high water table. In both of these regions, as in most places on the line, the Germans had chosen to entrench on what little high ground there was, further adding to the misery of the Allies, who were forced to build "trenches" above ground with massive lines of sandbags, sometimes as thick as 20 feet at the base and 10 feet at the top. Along the rest of the line it was possible to dig a standard trench in the earth, but the fight against water and subsidence was a constant one, even in the mountains at the very southern end of the Western Front.

All trenches, whether above or below ground, were built along the same basic design. The front of the trench was called the parapet and was ideally 10 feet high, thereby allowing men to walk along the length of the trench without fear of snipers. In order to see and fire out, there was a firestep of earth or sometimes wood that ran along the length of the trench. The back of the trench was called the parado. Both the parapet and the parado were topped with sandbags and shored up with revetments of logs, iron rebars, and more sandbags. The French often used wattle of interlaced branches and wicker.

Allied troops in 1916

French soldiers in a trench during the Battle of Verdun

Parapets often had steps called "sortie steps" cut into them to make it quick and easy for troops to go "over the top". A series of "grasping posts" set into the parapet gave the soldier something to grab onto while holding his rifle in his other hand, and large quantities of short ladders could be used as well. It was best to have men coming out all along the line rather than bunching up at a few sally points.

Generally, trenches were built on a zigzag pattern. This kept an explosion in one section of the trench from spreading shrapnel along the line, and it also isolated any breakthrough and kept attackers from firing down the length of the trench. There were usually three lines of trenches; the first was called the firing line, the second the support trench, and the third the reserve trench.

In parts of the line there may be more support trenches, often adding up to as many as 10 lines. Trenches were connected by communication trenches, also dug in a zigzag pattern, and latrines, dressing stations for the wounded, kitchens, and other necessary depots would be located in the communication trench.

A barber working on a soldier in a French trench

The British dug trenches in a jagged series of right angles to make a pattern similar to the crenellations atop a castle wall, with a section of about 10 feet sticking forward called a fire bay. Perpendicular sections connected them to stretches set a little further back, and these were called traverses. The Germans also adopted this technique.

Of course, this describes an ideal trench, but conditions on the ground often dictated otherwise. Muddy conditions and bombardment led to subsidence, heavy rain flooded entire areas, forcing the men to create new communication trenches. Sandbags would tear or get blown apart and needed constant replacing. Exhausted men may dig a trench to nonstandard proportions, and if an enemy trench was taken the survivors of the assault would then have to turn the parado into a parapet and add a firestep.

Extending out from the front or firing line were saps, narrow trenches running 20-30 yards out into No Man's Land to a small bay (often just a shell crater) where two or three men would sit listening at night for enemy movement. A French soldier remembered hating this duty, calling "the little listening posts of dreadful memory. It is difficult to imagine the suffering of the sentries…How often did the absolute solitude provoke panic at the slightest movement of an animal in the grass, at the stirring of a branch in the moonlight?"

The men considered sentry duty to be the worst task, as they were always tired thanks to long hours of manual labor and insufficient sleep for weeks on end. To be made to stand for hours at night, peering over the parapet or walking the rounds of the same short bit of dark trench, must have played on both minds and nerves. While the vast majority would struggle to do their duty and keep heavy eyelids open, some couldn't help but fall asleep, and the punishment for sleeping on sentry duty was death. A good officer or NCO would stop and chat with his sentries, which helped morale and helped keep them awake. The famous English author Robert Graves said of sentry duty, "At night our sentries had orders to stand with their head and shoulders above the parapet…It implied greater vigilance and self-confidence in the sentry, and also put the top of his head above the level of the parapet. Enemy machine guns were trained on this level, and it would be safer to get hit in the chest or shoulders than in the forehead."

Sentry duty was rotated with fatigue duty, during which the men would repair trenches, bring up food and supplies, and perform other such necessary tasks. Some jobs, like repairing exposed trenches, had to be done under the cover of night in order to reduce the chances of snipers or aerial observers.

With the Race to the Sea over, both sides dug in and the war of positioning was afoot. Offensives aimed to gain strategic points such as high ground or important railways close behind enemy lines. They would try to push back enemy salients or expand their own. Gone were the big sweeping movements across large sections of the map, even though the Allies never gave up hope of making a breakthrough.

At first, the French and British tried to break through with ever larger assaults. These would be preceded by heavy artillery bombardments in the hope that it would cut the German wire and destroy frontline defenses, but it rarely accomplished either objective. The Germans made some assaults as well, especially counterattacks against Allied salients, but the Germans already enjoyed the luxury of occupying French and Belgian territory, so they saw less of a need to go on the offensive. Paris was not going to be taken, and victory could be obtained by simply holding on.

There were also sudden surprise attacks without artillery preparation, which would often come just after dawn or just before dusk. Since the Allied trenches faced east, the rising sun would be in the solders' eyes, and the same held true for the sunset on the Germans. Thus, both sides had orders to "stand to" at these times, meaning all available troops not on essential duty would stand on the firestep and await an enemy attack.

As casualties mounted, commanders began to experiment with different types of attack formation. The Germans had already been trained to charge in open order to reduce casualties from shrapnel and machine guns, and their opponents adopted this practice too. In the first winter of the war, the Germans tried various other methods to break through enemy trenches, such as night attacks focused at certain points. If the men broke into the enemy trench, they'd work their way along it, killing the enemy as they went. Another technique was to bring machine guns and snipers close to the enemy trench and clear them with heavy fire, and by the end of 1915 both sides were making liberal use of grenades, with special parties of grenadiers, to clear out enemy trenches.

Picture of German soldiers charging in an open formation

Not surprisingly, snipers proved their importance in this new war of position. While most of the armies didn't have specialized snipers in 1914, those who had been marksmen in civilian life or who were army regulars with a special talent soon got the attention of their officers. The Germans were the first to use snipers in a systematic way. They were given camouflage, telescopic sights, and small metal shields with loopholes, but these shields soon proved a burden and were often disposed of by the men. Snipers were generally free of sentry and fatigue duty, and German snipers did not move with their units but stayed in the same sector for months on end, thereby becoming intimately familiar with the terrain.

Snipers on both sides often worked in pairs, with one man acting as a spotter and the other shooting. Snipers rarely stayed in the same place for long, instead moving around after a few shots and finding another vantage point, which kept them from becoming targets of sniper fire themselves. They also fired from craters or ruined buildings in No Man's Land, and some created fake trees with bulletproof shielding inside the trunks to hide inside. The Germans even tried flying kites with English writing on it so that when some foolish soldier popped his head above the parapet to try and read the words, he'd end up getting shot.

An Australian sniper team in a trench in 1915

Basic caution reduced the chance of being hit by a sniper, but getting rid of them proved difficult. One method was to have a few men watching a suspected sniper's nest while another man poked up a helmet on the end of a stick. If the sniper took the bait, he'd get several shots in his direction. More troublesome snipers could even attract a focused artillery barrage, and the lack of foresight can be seen in the fact that the men were not equipped with metal helmets to protect them when looking or firing over the parapet of a trench. Furthermore, artillery was provided with only a relatively small number of high-explosive shells. Instead, shrapnel shells were the most common type sent to the front, and they proved to have little effect against barbed wire (also in short supply in the opening months of the war) or against men hiding in entrenched positions.

The Germans were particularly good at building trenches and defensive positions, and when they had pulled back after the initial fighting in the early months of the war, they chose the best sites for their defensive lines. They also understood that in this war, once soldiers had dug in, the defense had the upper hand.

By early 1916, things had changed very little along the front, and neither side was able to make any progress for long. For this reason, Germany launched an attack in the area of Verdun, France. The strategy was to capture the high ground, which would give it a tactical advantage over the French army. The Germans believed the French would commit massive troops to regain their revered ancient city of Verdun.[1] In other words, the Germans had now begun a war of attrition in which they hoped to not win a battle as such, but to inflict more damage on their enemy than their enemy could inflict on them. Eventually, the thinking went, the French army would collapse and the Germans would be victorious.

Technically, Verdun was a French victory, but by the standards of any other conflict, people could be excused for considering it an unmitigated disaster for both sides. Much debate has centered around how many died at Verdun, and although the exact figures are unclear, it's clear that the combined French and German losses during those harrowing 10 months in 1916 amounted to over 700,000 killed, wounded, captured or missing (although some of the latter may well have deserted, it is likely that most were killed and never accounted for). Tens of millions of artillery shells were dropped, countless lives were lost or ruined, and all of it was over a patch of French countryside that was hardly different from countless others. After almost a year's fighting with a brutal intensity scarcely seen before or since in war, the French were masters of no more than the ground they had held at the start of the offensive. Much of the area itself would scarcely be recognizable as being on Earth, let alone part of the tranquil beauty of the French countryside.

It is difficult for words to convey the horrors of Verdun, and the other major battles on the Western Front for that matter. Shelling was a constant feature of daily life, but it was impossible to grow accustomed to the random, erratic fall of bombs which could strike either randomly or with seemingly deadly efficiency. The concentrated terror of a preliminary bombardment, when individual explosions merged into one long, continuous roar, is virtually unimaginable for anyone who hasn't experienced it. In addition to that, soldiers at Verdun had to worry about enemy snipers, machine gun fire, strafing runs from enemy fighter aircraft, and the dreaded poison gas which would leave men to asphyxiate slowly on the fluids from their ravaged lungs, choking like beached fish. The lottery of horrors was replete with grisly choices, and that was without factoring in the naked violence of hand-to-hand trench warfare, where rifle-butts and bayonets were practically merciful instruments of destruction compared to trench knives,

---

1   Foley, R. T. *German Strategy and the Path to Verdun: Erich von Falkenhayn and the Development of Attrition,* 1870–1916 (pbk. ed.). Cambridge: CUP., 2007, p. 192.

knuckledusters, entrenching spades with sharpened edges, clubs wrapped with barbed wire and studded with nails, and flame throwers. For those fortunate enough to avoid becoming a casualty in one of those ways, they still had to worry about diseases, from common flu and dysentery to more deadly problems like pneumonia, tuberculosis, and gangrenous wounds.

Even with frequent rotations away from the frontline, during which the French troops – but not their German counterparts – were able to get some respite from the unrelenting destruction, the psychological impact of the utter devastation all around was enormous. Millions of tons of high explosives ripped apart the landscape on a scale reminiscent of a nuclear holocaust. Woods were flattened or torn apart by shellfire, and what remained of them scavenged for firewood or to reinforce trenches. Villages and forts were reduced to piles of rubble that were scarcely recognizable as buildings. Any scrap of elevation was transformed into an artillery emplacement or, in some cases, battered down to ground level by constant shellfire. The ground itself was churned and truffled beyond all recognition, stripped completely of any blade of grass and turned into a muddy morass which clung to boots and into which soldiers sank to the knee. The landscape was pockmarked by shell-craters like the surface of the moon, and their sides were so slippery that soldiers who were unlucky enough to fall into them or dive into them for shelter from a barrage were unable to crawl out without help. In some cases, soldiers even drowned in the stagnant water that collected at the bottom of these holes. In winter, the ground froze solid and snow piled in high drifts in the trenches, adding frostbite and trenchfoot to the list of extreme miseries the soldiers were liable to suffer from.

A 2005 picture of part of the battlefield

Throughout the battle, corpses littered the landscape, as did broken or discarded equipment. Although attempts were made to bury the dead, both human and animal (thousands of horses, used for draft labor, also perished at Verdun), troops were often too exhausted to do so. If men were killed in no man's land, barring a truce to collect and bury the dead and tend to the wounded, there was no opportunity to attend to them, so they just rotted where they lay. No one would be foolish enough to risk sniper or machine gun fire to bury the dead, so they were forced to watch as bodies slowly fell apart in their uniforms, and the living had to endure the macabre stench of death. Soldiers who were killed in the opening hours of a multi-day offensive barrage were also liable to lie exposed in the trenches where they had been cut down for several days, their friends and comrades sheltering from the barrage just feet away watching them putrefy at their side. After an unsuccessful assault, the wounded who had the misfortune not to be rescued might scream in agony for days, shredding their comrades' nerves.

Verdun, like much of World War I, was combat at its most brutal and horrific, and it is easy to see why it continues to make a lasting impact on the French's collective memory. But in early 1916, when the British and French put together plans for an offensive at the Somme, they had no way of knowing what the final results at Verdun would entail. In fact, many of the Allied commanders feared that the German strategy was working and that the French army was in danger of collapse, so the purpose of the Allied attack at the Somme was to take pressure off the French army at Verdun in hopes the Germans would have to divert troops to the Somme to counter the Allied attack.[2]

With that in mind, General Haig, who commanded the British Expeditionary Force (BEF) and its new volunteer recruits, began to make plans for an offensive at the Somme.

Preparations for the Battle

Unfortunately for the Allied forces, when their drive to Paris failed, the Germans retreated and set up a line of trenches to secure their hold in France and exploit the resources in the land they had captured. They knew how to retreat in an orderly fashion and then to establish a place in the landscape that was to their benefit, which is exactly what they did at the Somme. They built an intricate front line of zig-zag trenches that was backed up by a network of reserve and support trenches. Most importantly, the trenches were dug out from hard chalk, a use of the natural strength of the land that would prove to be a brilliant strategy.

The Germans saw these trenches as somewhat permanent, so at the Somme, some rooms had electricity, ventilation, toilets, a bed, and even wallpaper.[3] They also picked a high point that gave them a commanding view of the opposing army, and the high terrain meant they had fewer problems with rain and drainage.

2   Haig, General Douglas, (D. HAIG, General, Commanding-in-Chief, British Armies in France). "Sir Douglas Haig's 2nd Despatch (Somme), 23 December 1916." https://www.firstworldwar.com/source/haigsommedespatch.htm. Accessed March 8, 2019.
3   Daniels, Patricia."History of Trench Warfare in World War I." ThoughtCo, August 13, 2018, www.thoughtco.com/trenches-in-world-war-i-1779981. Accessed March 8, 2019.

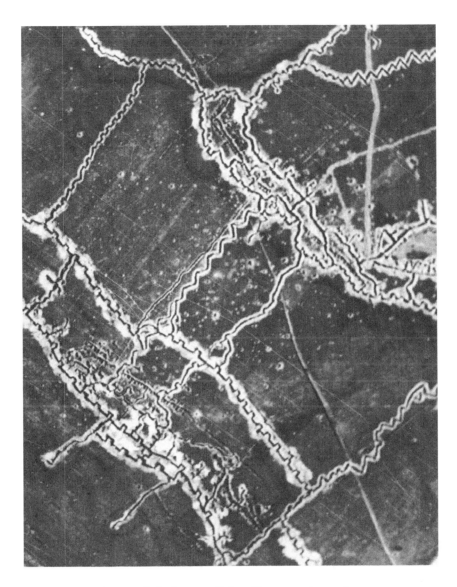

An aerial photo of the German trenches

A German soldier at the battle

Although General Haig did not understand the German trench system initially, in the following report six months after the start of the Battle of the Somme, he had at last grasped the strength of the German defenses: "During nearly two years' preparation [the Germans] had spared no pains to render these defences impregnable. The first and second systems each consisted of several lines of deep trenches, well provided with bomb-proof shelters and with numerous communication trenches connecting them. The front of the trenches in each system was protected by wire entanglements, many of them in two belts forty yards broad, built of iron stakes interlaced with barbed wire, often almost as thick as a man's finger."[4] By then, unfortunately, his lack of understanding at the beginning had resulted in the deaths of tens of thousands of young soldiers.

Haig and his allies, on the other hand, saw the trenches as temporary and thus had many more problems when it came to daily routines. Rain, drainage, and dampness were major problems, and if a man's foot never dried out, it could lead to gangrene and amputation. Even worse, about 100,000 men died due to trenchfoot by the end of the war. Rats were feeding off of corpses everywhere, and lice were always present.

---

4   Haig, 2nd Despatch (Somme).

When Britain declared war on Germany it had the largest navy in the world, but not much of an army. Thus, the call went out to entice young men to join the army and live the adventure. One famous poster featured a large old lion on a rock, surrounded by young male lions just below him

Lord Herbert Kitchener, the Secretary of State for War, wanted to put together a volunteer army starting soon after the "Rape of Belgium" and Britain's declaration of war with Germany. Known as The New Army or Kitchener's Volunteer Army or Kitchener's Mob, these soldiers came from working-class and middle-class backgrounds.

In a famous poster, Kitchener himself looked straight out at the viewer with his finger pointed at the viewer:

BRITONS

(Lord Kitchener)

WANTS YOU

JOIN YOUR COUNTRY'S ARMY!

GOD SAVE THE KING5

Kitchener initially wanted 500,000 volunteers, but he got 1.5 million, and these very young green soldiers had to be whipped into shape in time to go into battle in France. Many of these volunteers would see their first combat during the Battle of the Somme.

The British made the most of the "Rape of Belgium," working off the idea that if the Germans could do this to Belgium, they could do it to the rest of the world if they won the war. The British were morally indignant and used every propaganda ploy to get young men to enlist. Another poster showed a picture of a gorilla wearing a German helmet and holding a helpless half-naked woman in one arm and a club in the other.

DESTROY

5   File:30a Sammlung Eybl Großbritannien. Alfred Leete (1882–1933) Britons (Kitchener) wants you (Briten Kitchener braucht Euch). 1914 (Nachdruck), 74 x 50 cm. (Slg.Nr. 552).jpg. https://commons.wikimedia.org/wiki/File:30a_Sammlung_Eybl_Gro%C3%9Fbritannien._Alfred_Leete_(1882%E2%80%931933)_Britons_(Kitchener)_wants_you_(Briten_Kitchener_braucht_Euch)._1914_(Nachdruck),_74_x_50_cm._(Slg.Nr._552).jpg

THIS MAD BRUTE

ENLIST6

Perhaps the most effective poster was one of two women and a child looking proudly and somewhat sadly at their young men ready to go to war:

WOMEN OF BRITAIN

SAY -

"GO!"7

This seemingly quiet and simple poster was anything but. With Lord Kitchener's blessing,

6   File:Harry R. Hopps, Destroy this mad brute Enlist - U.S. Army, 03216u edit.jpg
     https://commons.wikimedia.org/wiki/File:Harry_R._Hopps,_Destroy_this_mad_brute_Enlist_
     -_U.S._Army,_03216u_edit.jpg

7   File:7 Collection Eybl Great Britain - E. Kealey - Women of Britain say – GO.jpg
     https://commons.wikimedia.org/wiki/File:7_Collection_Eybl_Great_Britain_-_E._Kealey_-
     _Women_of_Britain_say_%E2%80%93_GO.jpg

Admiral Charles Fitzgerald started the Order of the White Feather, or the "White Feather Movement" as it became known. He deputized women to give out white feathers to men who were not in uniform, and it quickly became a symbol of cowardice.

This practice spread like wildfire, and soon a large number of women across the country took it upon themselves to hand out white feathers. This all ensured that while the press portrayed the volunteer recruits as simply being brave and patriotic, a huge number were truly there because they had been intimidated. No doubt, many had to wonder if the defense of Belgium was worth the risks they would be taking.

Another method for attracting young men was the creation of "Pals Battalions," through which men from the same village could join and fight together. In the same vein, men who played football could join the Football Battalion. This seemed like a good idea and was condoned by those in command, operating under the assumption that men who knew each other or had the same interests could more easily adjust to both the difficulties of army life and the inevitable tragedies of combat.[8]

These Pal Battalions created social pressure as well, so when several men from a town joined, it motivated others to join in an effort to avoid being seen as unpatriotic or afraid of the dangers of battle.

Of course, there were patriotic songs encouraging young men to join the army. One stanza from the song *Fall In* by Harold Begbie (1914) went like this:

> "How will you fare, sonny, how will you fare
>
> In the far-off winter night
>
> When you sit by the fire in the old man's chair
>
> And your neighbours talk of the fight?
>
> Will you slink away, as it were from a blow,
>
> Your old head shamed and bent?
>
> Or say, 'I was not with the first to go,
>
> But I went, thank God, I went?"[9]

---

8   "Pals Battalions" ("BATTLE OF THE SOMME"). Yorkshire Reporter, November 7, 2016, www.yorkshirereporter.co.uk/zyxc/battle-of-the-somme/. Accessed March 8, 2019.

9   Begbie, Harold. "Fall In." Lyrics quoted by George Upton in his book *The Song: Its Birth, Evolution, and Functions*. Chicago, A.C. McClurg & Co., 1915, p. 100.

While the British officials were glad for the huge volunteer response, they were also overwhelmed, and they needed seasoned older men who knew the ropes and who could train these green recruits. Since 1880, school had been compulsory in England, so even the working class boys were used to being taught and taking orders from their teachers. From all reports, the British did a remarkable job of organizing this flood of men and getting them used to military discipline and the potential hardships of trench warfare. As a result, when the men arrived at the Somme, they believed they were adequately trained and adjusted to the army way of life, and they were eager to fight.

The area of the Somme River in France was chosen for an attack on German trench positions by the French in part because the British could land on the western French coast and bring in supplies and then work next to the French army, which would join them and take part in the offense on the eastern side of the operation. Originally, the French planned to commit a large number of troops, but due to the fighting at Verdun, they would be ultimately be unable to do so. This meant that the British and General Haig took over and were essentially in command of the entire operation.

Haig

The logistics of the British presence at the Somme were mindboggling, and it is doubtful that any other general could have organized it so well and kept a handle on the thousands of tons of supplies, the building of railroad tracks, and the command of a young untried volunteer army that was still being trained. In addition, the supply of water to the troops was a major concern - 120 miles of water mains had to be constructed.10

In late 1915, French Commander in Chief Joseph Joffre had put together a plan for a joint French-English operation, to which Haig agreed. While the British eventually took over most everything, the French still played a major role, and they insisted that the start of the attack be moved up from August 1 to July 1 to help relieve forces at Verdun. Haig was happy to be the

---

10 Haig, 2nd Despatch (Somme).

commander of these troops, but he preferred to start an offensive at a different location and only after his troops had more training. In addition, he would have to start a month earlier than originally planned and would not get nearly as much support as he had been promised by the French.

The First Day on the Somme

On December 23, 1916, Haig reported to General Headquarters:

"The object of that offensive was threefold

To relieve the pressure on Verdun.

To assist our Allies in the other theatres of war by stopping any further transfer of German troops from the Western front.

To wear down the strength of the forces opposed to us."11

This statement of war objectives in December 1916 restated the plan that had been originally formulated in early 1916 by Haig and Joffre. However, in his summary at the end of the year, General Haig left out an important point: he had changed the original plan and included an additional objective which had led to the slaughter on the first day of the Battle of the Somme.

The initial plan of attack had been put together by Lieutenant-General Henry Rawlinson. Originally, the line that would be attacked was much shorter, and a tremendous British artillery bombardment was to be aimed at the German trenches at the front of the line. However, Haig changed this by extending the line and insisting that the artillery attack the second line of trenches as well.

A British battery at the battle

The British had planned on unleashing the largest artillery bombardment in the history of the British military, and in the eight days leading up to the attack, they fired more than 1.5 million

---

11 Haig, 2nd Despatch (Somme).

shells from about 1,500 guns. That said, more important than the number of shells was the number of " shells per yard." Haig had cut the impact of these shells in half, and this miscalculation would cost his men dearly. On the day of the attack, they would discover that the shelling had not done nearly as much damage as they had anticipated.12

Haig had made these changes because he optimistically envisioned the possibility of a breakthrough, and as a cavalryman himself, he had cavalry ready to pounce if the infantry was able to cut through the German trenches and open up a path. Of course, just about all of the lessons taught by the war to date demonstrated that cavalry was no longer effective, and it would be no different at the Somme.13

At the beginning of the battle, Haig had almost 400,000 men in 13 divisions, while the Germans had a little more than 300,000 men in about 10 divisions. Soon after the battle started, more troops would be added to both sides, resulting in almost 1.5 million men on each side in 50 divisions each. This in itself achieved one of the Allied Powers' central aims, which was to compel the transfer of German soldiers from Verdun to take pressure off the French. The British also could lean on troops from their colonies, and their army fielded soldiers from Canada, India, South Africa, Australia, New Zealand, and even Bermuda.

At precisely 7:30 am on July 1, 1916, British soldiers from Lord Kitchener's Volunteer army went "over the top" out of their trenches and into No Man's Land, the deadliest area imaginable in World War I. They walked slowly in step as they had been ordered and were told to keep going forward no matter what. Retreat was not an option, but everyone from the officers down to the soldiers believed that the week-long shelling had pulverized the German trenches and that they would meet little opposition.

Due to communication problems at this point in the war, the attack was planned by the minute. This meant that the artillery would keep firing until they could see by their watches that the attacking infantry was scheduled to be close to the German front lines. This is why the soldiers left the trenches at exactly 7:30, and why they walked at a measured pace. Unfortunately, it turned out that just about every assumption the British officers had made ahead of the fighting would prove incorrect.

In hindsight, the first day of what became the war's largest battle appears to be an unusually odd event. Untested volunteer soldiers came up against an entrenched and well-armed

12 Baker, Chris. "British artillery bombardment before the infantry attack on the Somme." THE LONG, LONG TRAIL, 2019, www.longlongtrail.co.uk/battles/battles-of-the-western-front-in-france-and-flanders/the-battles-of-the-somme-1916/british-artillery-bombardment-before-the-infantry-attack-on-the-somme/. Accessed March 8, 2019.

13 Walsh, Ben. "The Plan" ("The Somme > Background"). The National Archives, www.nationalarchives.gov.uk/education/greatwar/g4/cs3/background.htm. Accessed March 8, 2019.

professional enemy who had not been badly affected by one of the largest bombardments ever unleashed, which meant element of surprise was with the defenders positioned in a perfect place to do the most damage.

That's exactly what the Germans accomplished on July 1. Using their formidable machine gun tactics, the Germans showered the soldiers with interlocking bullets that were inescapable.14 Their guns were part of a network that could be aimed close by or indirectly hundreds of meters away, just like artillery, and the guns could be networked to fire at any angle. The British had not given the machine gun much credibility, but the Somme taught them quite quickly. In his report several months after the fighting started, Haig wrote, "These various [machine gun] systems of defence, with the fortified localities and other supporting points between them, were cunningly sited to afford each other mutual assistance and to admit of the utmost possible development of enfilade and flanking fire by machine guns and artillery. They formed, in short, not merely a series of successive lines, but one composite system of enormous depth and strength."15

Indeed, the British did not understand how the Germans were using their machine guns in this manner. Combined with barbed wire that was as thick as a man's finger and German high explosive artillery rounds that sprayed splinters down upon the enemy soldiers, there was no escape.

---

14 Haig, 2nd Despatch (Somme).
15 Haig, 2nd Despatch (Somme).

A picture of British soldiers advancing

In a matter of hours, 19,240 enthusiastic young men who marched off to war full of idealistic notions lay dead in No Man's Land. Many men from the same town in the Pals Battalions were mowed down together, and aside from the dead, another 40,000 were wounded. Needless to say, the stretcher bearers were overwhelmed, as were the doctors and nurses who had expected far fewer casualties. For those who were still alive between the lines, it took as long as four days to reach the hospital.

Initial Reactions to the First Day

A famous anecdote about the war is that a German officer, in response to being told how hard the British soldiers fought, claimed that the soldiers were "lions led by donkeys." That said, while General Haig has taken much of the blame for the day's carnage and for continuing the attack the next day, there were other factors at play. In fact, it seems that he did not know the full extent of the slaughter until four days after the fighting, because it took that long to gather up and tally up the dead, wounded and missing.[16] Furthermore, the first day had not been a total loss, and Haig believed there were a number of successes to exploit in the days to come.

Ahead of the advance, there were 18 different mining operations, and most of them were successful. Huge explosions occurred right next to the German front lines, marking the moment the British soldiers poured out to attack. In addition, the French made good progress on the southern end of the line during the fighting on July 1.

---

16 Whitehead, R. J. *The Other Side of the Wire: The Battle of the Somme. With the German XIV Reserve Corps, 1 July 1916. II. Solihull: Helion.* 2013, p. 476.

A picture of a mine explosion during the first day

Haig attempted to exploit this potential opening on July 2, and over the coming weeks, the British would take about 7.5 miles of German territory. This wedge of territory was positioned so well that Haig believed it would lead to a breakthrough in the spring.

No breakthrough would come in 1917, and the fact of the matter is that a number of things went wrong for the British from the very beginning. Moreover, as the battle progressed, it should have been obvious that things were not going according to plan, and that the strategy needed to be reconsidered. This would be standard operating procedure in any unexpected situation, and even more so when so many men's lives were at stake.

The first mistaken assumption was that a massive artillery bombardment would clear out the front line and allow British troops to almost walk unharmed across No Man's Land. Given the quality of the gunners and the sheer number of shells fired, Rawlinson believed that "nothing could exist at the conclusion of the bombardment in the area covered by it." For that reason, the generals assumed the assault on the German front lines could literally be accomplished with a "walk."[17]

_____

17 Baker, "British artillery bombardment before the infantry attack on the Somme."

However, alongside the fact that Haig had lengthened the line of attack and diluted the effect of the shelling, the Germans had built solid bunkers deep down in the hard chalk that allowed them to wait out the bombardment. When the shelling stopped, German soldiers simply came "up top" to their trenches and went back into action.

The British didn't seem to consider such a contingency, which is all the more tragic given that their trenches were made from the same soil. While they did not have the prime spot that the Germans had, it should've been apparent to them that trenches made from chalk could withstand the effects of an artillery bombardment much better than ones simply made from dirt. Making matters worse, the German machine guns had been placed in well-designed concrete pillboxes, which survived the bombing, and their telephone communications were not disrupted because the Germans had carefully buried the wires. Another assumption was that the shelling would destroy the barbed wire, but in many cases, the explosions simply passed through the heavy barbed wire. In fact, in some places, it just tangled the wire more.

Haig had altered the plan because he believed he could break through the German lines with his cavalry, and he made no secret of this. By doing so, however, he fundamentally altered the objectives of the plan, which were to inflict as much damage as possible on the enemy. The original plan by Rawlinson was much better suited for that task, but as journalist Phillip Gibbs put it, "Haig as a cavalryman was obsessed with the idea that he would break the German line and send the cavalry through. It was a fantastic hope, ridiculed by the German High Command in their report on the Battles of the Somme which afterwards we captured."[18]

As it turned out, there was a very troubling defect in the artillery shells themselves. About a third of the shells fired were duds, which meant the British calculations were that much further off.[19]

The massive artillery bombardment was a giveaway that a general attack was forthcoming, but for a variety of other reasons, the Germans knew an attack was imminent. For months, they had observed the huge buildup of forces opposing them, and the ferocity of the bombardment suggested that the attack would begin immediately after the end of the shelling. Thus, when the shelling stopped a few minutes after 7:30 a.m. on July 1, the Germans quickly jumped out of their bunkers and manned their machine guns and rifles before the enemy infantry was even close. The Germans were not only in place but prepared for this moment.

If being prepared atop high ground wasn't enough advantage for the Germans, the action on the first day ensured that while the defense could establish a solid network of telephone communication via wires, the attackers could not. Clearly, the British soldiers and officers

18 Gibbs, Philip. Journalist quoted in *Reporting from the Front: War Reporters During the Great War* by Brian Best. Pen and Sword, Nov 30, 2014, p. 91.
19 Baker, "British artillery bombardment before the infantry attack on the Somme."

suffered through the fog of war, and had they been aware of the carnage in real time, the plans may have been changed. General Haig made this reference to the terrible losses of untried troops: "We were compelled either to use hastily trained and inexperienced officers and men or else to defer the offensive until we had trained them. In this latter case, we should have failed our Allies. That these troops should have accomplished so much under such conditions, and against an Army and a nation whose chief concern for so many years has been preparation for war, constitutes a feat of which the history of our nation records no equal."[20]

Meanwhile, the following news report is what people read back in England about the start of the Battle of the Somme a few days later: "A perceptible slackening of our fire soon after seven was the first indication given to us that our gallant soldiers were about to leap from their trenches and advance against the enemy. Non-combatants, of course, were not permitted to witness this spectacle, but I am informed that the vigour and eagerness of the first assault were worthy of the best tradition of the British Army. We had not to wait long for news, and it was wholly satisfactory and encouraging. The message received at ten o'clock ran something like this: "On a front of twenty miles north and south of the Somme, we and our French allies have advanced and taken the German first line of trenches. We are attacking vigourously Fricourt, la Boiselle and Mametz. German prisoners are surrendering freely, and a good many already fallen into our hands."[21]

George Coppard, a machine gunner at the battle, described his experience in the aftermath of the first day: "The next morning (July 2nd) we gunners surveyed the dreadful scene in front of us......it became clear that the Germans always had a commanding view of No Man's Land. (The British) attack had been brutally repulsed. Hundreds of dead were strung out like wreckage washed up to a high water-mark. Quite as many died on the enemy wire as on the ground, like fish caught in the net. They hung there in grotesque postures. Some looked as if they were praying; they had died on their knees and the wire had prevented their fall. Machine gun fire had done its terrible work."[22]

All that people knew in early July was what was reported in government approved documents, so there was almost no indication of the slaughter that had taken place. By the second week in July, however, the War Office Weekly Casualty Lists were published in newspapers, and the

---

20 Haig, 2nd Despatch (Somme).
21 Irvine, John. Report in the "Daily Express" on July 3rd 1916. Reprinted by
   C N Trueman "The Battle Of The Somme." The History Learning Site, Apr 2015,
   www.historylearningsite.co.uk/world-war-one/battles-of-world-war-one/the-battle-of-the-
   somme/17. Accessed March 8, 2019.
22 Coppard, George. Quote from a machine gunner at the Battle of the Somme. Reprinted by
   C N Trueman "The Battle Of The Somme." The History Learning Site, Apr 2015,
   www.historylearningsite.co.uk/world-war-one/battles-of-world-war-one/the-battle-of-the-
   somme/17. Accessed March 8, 2019.

extent of the horror gradually became apparent in the coming weeks. Since the soldiers in the Pals Battalions had stayed together, an entire generation of young men in many small towns was affected. The Leeds Pals of West Yorkshire Regiment lost 248 men, and it was reported that on every street in Leeds there was one home with curtains drawn. The Accrington Pals suffered the worst, with 584 casualties out of the 720 men in the battalion.[23]

While no one spoke out against the war, local impromptu memorial shrines appeared in towns across the country. One woman recalled, "The usual form was a simple triptych, with a shelf beneath for flowers, recording the names of all who had gone out from the street to serve the Colours. They quickly proved of real spiritual value."[24]

In mid-August, a silent movie about the Battle of the Somme came to theaters across England. An Official War Film,[25] this movie was shot during the preparations at the Somme and during some of the early fighting. The footage was real and powerful. Movies were still relatively new in 1916, and audiences were seeing actual soldiers on the battlefield. It would have been difficult at the time to not feel a sense of pride over the dedication the soldiers exhibited. About 20 million people in Britain saw the film and were inspired by it, and to many, it confirmed the rightness of the English cause and the necessity for sacrifice. David Lloyd George wrote that citizens should "see that this picture, which is in itself an epic of self-sacrifice and gallantry, reaches everyone. Herald the deeds of our brave men to the ends of the earth. This is your duty."[26] On the poster for the movie was a quote from Lloyd George, telling viewers, "If the exhibition of this Picture all over the world does not end War, God help civilisation!"

23 "Pals Battalions" ("BATTLE OF THE SOMME"). Yorkshire Reporter, November 7, 2016, www.yorkshirereporter.co.uk/zyxc/battle-of-the-somme/. Accessed March 8, 2019.

24 Howse, Christopher. "Shrines built while the First World War went on." THE TELEGRAPH, Jun 2009, www.telegraph.co.uk/comment/columnists/christopherhowse/5581520/Shrines-built-while-the-First-World-War-went-on.html. Accessed March 8, 2019.

25 The Battle of the Somme (1916 film), Official War Film, distributed by British Topical Committee for War Films. Available at: https://www.youtube.com/watch?v=xQ_OZfaiUlc. Accessed March 8, 2019.

26 Badsey, S. (1983). "Battle of the Somme: British War-Propaganda". Historical Journal of Film, Radio and Television. 3 (2): 99 doi:10.1080/01439688300260081. ISSN 0143-9685.

On August 22, 1916, *The Times* reported, "Crowded audiences ... were interested and thrilled to have the realities of war brought so vividly before them, and if women had sometimes to shut their eyes to escape for a moment from the tragedy of the toll of battle which the film presents, opinion seems to be general that it was wise that the people at home should have this glimpse of what our soldiers are doing and daring and suffering in Picardy."[27]

In reality, the movie misrepresented the actual conditions at the Somme. The upbeat movie, which showed hordes of German prisoners being taken and treated well, along with attentive doctors and nurses quickly tending to the wounded, was quite simply a propaganda ploy. It was designed to focus people's attention on victory and the best of British morality while obscuring the horrific carnage.

It has been documented that some British soldiers took no prisoners,[28] and that many wounded who might have survived ended up dying because they were not treated in time. Many German prisoners were taken, but there were many more British killed and wounded than Germans at the start of the battle. The battle was notorious for rainy conditions that made the land muddy and

---

27 "War's Realities on the Cinema". The Times. London. 22 August 1916. ISSN 0140-0460.
28 Comments in the Great War Forum. "Taking no prisoners."
   https://www.greatwarforum.org/topic/78568-taking-no-prisoners/. Accessed March 8, 2019.

difficult, but the footage in the movie showed only good weather.

Attempting to Break the Stalemate

After the horrific opening day, Haig did not flinch and continued to order offensive operations, although the focus now was not so much on a breakthrough as he had originally hoped, but more of a piecemeal approach. He avoided attacking the area in the north where the casualties had been the heaviest and instead concentrated on areas in the south where the French had more success on the first day.

The British army proceeded in a methodical fashion and gradually carved out a wedge of about 7.5 miles over the next five months, which historians tend to divide into three phases. The gains ultimately cost about 415,000 British casualties and about 200,000 French casualties, the equivalent of 50 casualties per yard gained, but both Haig and the Germans believed those gains put the British in an advantageous position that could lead to a breakthrough. Haig would only stop his operations in November because of snow and bad weather, and he planned to resume his attack in the spring, but the Germans withdrew back to their new defensive Hindenburg Line before he could attack again. As they rightly anticipated, their position at the Somme could not be held.

The five months of battle were divided into three phases. The offensive that began on the first day was part of what became known as the Battle of Albert. The first day of fighting allowed the Allies to gain a foothold on the southern front, and from there, Haig concentrated his offense on this southern portion and avoided the northern high points. From July 14-17, the British were more successful in using artillery ahead of the Battle of Bazentin Ridge, allowing the infantry to reach the front lines before being fired upon. On July 19, however, Australian soldiers within the army suffered one of the worst days in Australian military history at the Battle of Fromelles.

By the middle of the month, the Germans began to move large numbers of troops from the Battle of Verdun over to the Somme. Meanwhile, the two sides fought the Battle of Delville Wood from July 14 into September, which took place among fortified villages and high ground that allowed the British to target their artillery. By this time, the Allies had learned to use indirect machine gun fire effectively, and at one point during the fighting, 10 Vickers machine guns saturated an area about a mile away for 12 hours. [29]

In the Battle of Pozières, fought from July 23-August 7, the Australians took the town of Pozières and eventually captured the important high ground next to the village.

In early September, the village of Guillemont was captured, but then a lack of coordination between the French and English generals prevented further gains. When these armies paused, the

---

[29] Hogg, Ian and Batchelor, John. *Weapons & War Machines.* New York, Crescent Books, 1975.

Germans launched their largest counterattack.

On September 9, the German-held town of Ginchy was captured, as was the area around it. This gave the British a much better position to launch attacks from, and it would result in large losses for the German defenders.

In the Air

"During my whole life I have not found a happier hunting ground than in the course of the Somme battle."30 – The Red Baron

One of the most important breakthroughs in military technology associated with World War I, and certainly the one that continues to capture the public imagination, was the use of airplanes, which were a virtual novelty a decade before. While the war quickly ground to a halt in its first few months, the skies above the Western Front became increasingly busy. The great powers had already been acquiring aircraft for potential uses, but given that aerial warfare had never been a major component of any conflict, it's understandable that few on either side had any idea what the planes were capable of doing. Furthermore, at the start of the war, all sides' aircraft were ill-equipped for combat mostly because the idea that planes might somehow fight was still a novel one, and the adaptations had not yet been developed that would allow the aerial battles later in the war.

As a result, aircraft were used almost entirely for reconnaissance early on, allowing generals to gain unprecedented levels of information about enemy movements. Such intelligence allowed the French to counter German movements in what became the First Battle of the Marne, ending Germany's hopes for victory through the Schlieffen plan. Similarly, in the east, German planes were vital in tracking, encircling and destroying Russian forces at Tannenberg.

Some armies, such as the French, saw air intelligence as a strategic matter, with aircraft capable mainly of identifying enemy forces before battle and contributing to advanced preparations. The Germans, on the other hand, believed that aircraft could provide tactical information once battle had commenced. Pilots such as Oswald Boelcke, Germany's first great aerial officer, would fly over enemy positions in two-seat aircraft with a spotter in the back, identifying Allied positions and using colored lights to direct the fire of artillery on the ground.

Of course, spotting took on great importance because of the growing range and power of artillery. Much of the fire from the great guns was aimed indirectly since the gunners could not see their targets and thus relied on intelligence from others to direct them. Maps of enemy-held territory were often woefully inadequate to start with, and with the need to know where moving enemy formations were positioned, the business gained an added complexity, but aircraft could

---

30 von Richthofen, Captain Manfred Freiherr. *The Red Battle Flyer.* Translated by Ellis Barker, M. Dent & Sons, Ltd. Toronto, Canada, 1918.

cut through this by providing up-to-date intelligence on enemy positions and sending it back to the gun batteries which were lobbing shells over their own front lines.

The Royal Air Force (RAF), Britain's legendary air arm, was born in the skies above the First World War. The British had previously used balloons for spotting and reconnaissance for decades, and in the years leading up to the war, planes started seeing military use. They mostly provided reconnaissance, though experiments were made in using them offensively. During the Boer War of 1899-1902, the British Army used the crews of helium-filled balloons to plot and help target artillery fire. But these were small, tentative steps. The first patent to fit a machine gun to a plane, taken out in 1910, had not yet led to active fighting vehicles, and there was no doctrine, no tactics, and no combat between massed air fleets.

Everything would change near the start of World War I. Along with the technology, the tactics of aerial combat were also developing fast, and with its consequences of victory or death, fighting provided a good motive to learn better approaches fast. Oswald Boelcke, who without official permission had taken Fokker's plane for its first real outing, took the lead in developing the tactics that would make the Fokker plane invaluable. Staying on the German side of the lines, he used clouds and the glare of the sun to disguise his approach before shooting enemy planes down with short, accurate bursts of fire at close range. He paid attention not just to the workings of his machine but to those of his opponents, learning the design and limitations of captured Allied planes and determining the capabilities of their guns and where their blind spots lay. He also collaborated with the German anti-aircraft gunners on the ground, who provided him with warning shots when he was in danger and covering fire when he was under attack.

Boelcke

One of Boelcke's colleagues, Max Immelmann, added a sophisticated high speed maneuver to the German arsenal. The Immelmann turn, the first true air-to-air tactical maneuver, allowed the Fokker planes to attack their enemies again and again in quick succession, adding to their dominance as long as the enemy flew inferior planes. Its success helped earn its inventor his nickname "The Eagle of Lille," but this superiority only lasted until the following spring, when the Allied Powers developed and installed their own version of the Fokker technology. With that adaptation, the maneuver that had given Germans dominance now became a hazard to its own users.

Immelmann

Furthermore, Boelcke and Immelmann introduced the formation which has been the basis of fighter groups ever since: the pair of fighters. Boelcke realized that hunting out targets required a dangerous amount of attention; after all, while he was focused on stalking a single plane, others could approach without him noticing it. This meant the tactics which brought him success were also putting his life in danger. He therefore teamed up with Immelmann, the two guarding and protecting each other. The radios of the time were too heavy and cumbersome to install in an aircraft, so the pilots signaled to each other by waggling the wings of their planes, with Boelcke as the leader deciding when to attack and when to break off.

The British spent the early years of the war behind the Germans tactically and technologically. It was not until the summer of 1915 that they fielded their first dedicated fighter units, consisting of the Vickers F.B.5s. The summer of 1915 also saw a change in leadership for the air force, as

Major-General Sir Hugh Trenchard took over from Major-General Sir David Henderson as the commander of the force. This would prove to be a turning point, and Trenchard went on to shape the future Royal Air Force.

Trenchard

Even as these developments occurred in real time, the equipment for both pilots and planes remained incredibly primitive by later standards. The cockpits of the planes were not enclosed with glass as they would be in the Second World War, leaving air crews exposed to the elements as they flew, battered by cold, wind, and rain. Inside the cockpit, there were relatively few instruments; dials indicated height, airspeed, fuel, and oil pressure, but everything else, the location of enemy aircraft to the state of the plane, had to be judged by sight and sound.

Radios were also a rarity. In the days before transistors, a wireless set could weigh 250 pounds, a significant drag on the speed and maneuverability of a plane, which was something that fighter pilots could seldom afford. The radios that were installed usually sent and received Morse code rather than audio signals, meaning that they had to be operated by hand and the results decoded. 300 feet of aerial had to be trailed behind early radio-equipped planes, thanks to the wave-lengths they used, and this was another reason why they were impractical in planes taking part in the fast, swirling mess of dogfights.

All the while, both sides were making significant steps forward in aircraft design. One of the biggest was the widespread adoption of the interrupter gear for machine guns as the Allies mastered this German technology, but another important step forward came in engine design. At the start of the war, 80% of military planes had engines derived from a single model. This was the rotary engine that Louis Blériot had used in his groundbreaking flight across the English Channel in 1909. It had a good ratio of power to weight, a crucial factor in high performance combat planes, but it also had significant problems. As they revolved around the central crankshaft, the cylinders created a huge amount of torque. This twisting motion made planes powered by a rotary engine harder to handle and it was a problem that only increased with the power of the engines.

Blériot

Of course, powerful engines were what everybody wanted. The speed and efficiency of aircraft depended upon a balance between the power of the engine and the weight of the plane. The planes, mostly made of canvas over wooden frames, were already as light and flimsy as they could be without causing serious problems. As engineers improved their understanding of aerodynamics, shapes could be improved, but the onus for improvement fell primarily on the engines.

The answer was a shift towards stationary radial, inline, or V-engines, which escaped the serious torque problems. Aircraft engineers turned their attention to creating more powerful versions of these engines, leading to a fourfold increase in their power by the end of the war. This led to a series of better and better planes, and the balance of the war in the air swung back and forth as first one side and then the other gained dominance with a new weapon.

For the British, the first game changer was the de Havilland DH2. The RFC's Number 24 Squadron arrived in France in February 1916 with these new planes, the first British single-seater fighter. The DH2 was a pusher plane and challenging to fly, but it paid off the patience of the men who learnt how. They broke the superiority of the dreaded Eindecker, ending the Fokker Scourge. For the first time, the British had the upper hand in the air.

The DH2

The DH2 was followed in April by another important plane, the Sopwith 1 1/2 Strutter. This was the first British plane purposely designed to be mounted with a synchronised forward firing machine gun, using the interrupter gear. Over 1,500 of these planes saw use during the war, and it provided the layout upon which many other British biplanes were based. Among these was the Sopwith Pup, which came in later in the year, of which over 5,000 would be made.

With their air superiority, the Allies threw hundreds of pilots into supporting the bloody ground offensive on the Somme, and in doing so greatly supported their war effort. The British were hurling men and planes into the meat grinder, putting little effort into providing training and experience before they did so, but in the broader scope of the war, this was supporting their aims.

Later in 1916, the Germans regained the edge with the Albatros D.III plane, and the see-saw of military technological advantage swayed back and forth. Industrial programs were increasingly important when it came to providing both new technology and large amounts of material for aerial combat, and the Germans were not yet suffering from the shortages that would later hamper them.

The Albatros D.III

It was in this context that the most famous combat pilot in history, Manfred von Richthofen, made his presence felt over the Somme. It's only fair to point out that the Red Baron's rise to prominence came in part because of the loss of the greats who had come before him. Death was common for fliers, and often terrible. There were no parachutes, and the best hope of surviving a damaged plane was a risky crash landing. If the plane caught fire then the pilot would often jump to his death rather than die in a cockpit inferno. These young officers were avoiding the now infamous horrors of trench warfare, but they faced their own sort of terror.

The Red Baron

Manfred von Richthofen was invited to join the most prestigious air unit of the war to date, Boelcke's new Jasta 2, and the unit saw the first in its long string of successes on September 17, 1916, during the fighting on the Somme. In this fighting, von Richthofen scored his own first success, shooting down a British F.E.2b of Number 11 Squadron and mortally wounding Second Lieutenant Morris and Lieutenant Rees, the men in the plane. Like Boelcke, von Richthofen brought a hunter's instincts to the skies. Ruthless, patient, and calculating, he stalked his prey through the air, using sun, wind and cloud cover to gain an advantage of position and descend upon them with deadly power and suddenness. The Red Baron once asserted, "During my whole life I have not found a happier hunting ground than in the course of the Somme Battle. In the morning, as soon as I had got up, the first Englishmen arrived, and the last did not disappear until long after sunset. Boelcke once said that this was the El Dorado of the flying men."

As it turned out, Von Richthofen took part in the battle on October 28 in which his commander and hero was killed. Boelcke and another pilot, Erwin Boehme, were diving after a British D.H.2 plane of Number 24 Squadron, but another D.H.2, under fire from von Richthofen, burst across their line of sight. Boelcke banked away and Boehme swerved, resulting in the two colliding with each other. The struts and upper wing of Boelcke's plane collapsed and broke away, the plane fell into a spin, and it crashed into the ground near Bapaume. In the whirling chaos of combat, Richthofen had unwittingly played a part in bringing about Boelcke's demise.

Jasta 2 was renamed Jasta Boelcke by imperial decree, in honor of the man who had done so much to shape Germany's fledgling air force. Lieutenant Stephen Kirmaier took command following the master's death, but he too died in action less than a month later and was followed by Hauptmann Waltz.

Meanwhile, von Richthofen soon built up an impressive string of victories. On November 23, he took down one of the leading British flying aces, Victoria Cross holder Major L. G. Hawker, his 11th kill. With Hawker crashing behind enemy lines, Richthofen was able to salvage one of his plane's guns and kept it as a proud trophy. It was a credo in line with one of his most famous quotes: "I honored the fallen enemy by placing a stone on his beautiful grave."

Hawker

Of course, part of the reason the Red Baron found such a "happy hunting ground" over the Somme is because of the sheer resources the British threw into the theater. From July-November 1916, 308 British airmen died, were wounded, or went missing during the battle, nearly five times as many men as they had planes at the start of the war. To make up for these losses, there was a campaign to recruit new pilots. Some came from civilian life, called to arms to defend their country in its time of crisis. Others transferred from other military services, attracted by the glamour of the fighter aces. 1,300 men a month went through pilot training, but such was the rush to get them into combat that their flying course was only 18 hours long.

More significant than the shortage of pilots was the shortage of technicians. For every plane in the air, 47 ground staff were needed to keep it up and running, and no matter how hard the RFC pushed, they couldn't produce enough skilled staff to meet the needs of their ever-expanding aerial armada. Training for mechanics was brought together in one place at Halton Park to try to make up for this, and the Women's Royal Air Force was also founded to try to make up for shortages of support staff.

The Tanks at the Somme

To this day, modern warfare remains synonymous with tanks and mass infantry battles, although a confrontation of this nature has not occurred (except briefly during Operation Desert Storm) since World War II.

As a concept, it was not revolutionary; in fact, it harkened back to classical antiquity and to the Middle Ages, such as the covered battering rams and *testudos* which had made frequent appearances on ancient battlefields. In essence, it was designed to solve the age-old problem of protecting infantry from enemy projectiles while remaining mobile.

The development of both modern artillery and machine guns, as well as the stalemate engendered by heavy fortifications and entrenchments, had hamstrung the mobility of infantry and cavalry and also left them both utterly vulnerable to defensive firepower. Since they were incapable of replying in kind, the tank was designed to bridge that gap. The tank's armor, thick enough to withstand lateral fragmentation from exploding shells (although not direct hits) also made it virtually invulnerable to enemy rifle and machine gun fire, and its large tread meant that it could bridge trenches which would, at the very least, have delayed infantry substantially. As for the barbed wire entanglements and obstacles that severely delayed infantry and exposed them to enemy fire, tanks could simply drive right through it.

Various armies had flirted with the concept of a tank prior to World War I, but advances in metallurgical techniques (allowing for suitably solid and relatively lightweight armor) and in mechanical engineering (which allowed for the construction of a powerful engine capable of driving such a mass) finally made its development and deployment possible, as did the development of treaded track (initially for agricultural use in tractors). It was the British (at the instigation of Winston Churchill) who pioneered the "landship", but the French soon followed suit with their own designs. Ironically, Germany, which would subsequently become famous for panzers and blitzkrieg warfare, was late in taking up the idea. During World War I, the Germans continued to rely on other techniques, and they produced less than two dozen models for battlefield use.

The tanks of World War I, revolutionary (and initially terrifying) as they were, had their limitations. A standard tank would literally consume its own weight in spare parts, and they were painfully slow compared to more modern iterations. They were also lightly armed – usually with machine guns or light guns at most – and some poorly designed models tended to "ditch" themselves, sometimes irretrievably, in wider trenches. However, as a mobile bastion for infantry to shelter behind in the advance, and as a psychological weapon, they were significant.

The most iconic tank of World War I, the Mark I (which later went through several iterations, although only Mark I-IV saw combat during the war), was employed by a number of armies. The Mark I was produced by a specially designed government committee with the full cooperation of all services and British industry, resulting in a cohesive and practical whole. Over 30 feet long and weighing just under 30 tons, the Mark I came in two versions: a "male" (armed with side-mounted turret guns) and a "female" that didn't have the guns. Crewed by 8 men, it could achieve the rather unspectacular speed of 4 miles per hour, and its 60-gallon tank gave it an operational radius of just under 24 miles thanks to its thirsty Daimler-Knight 6-cylinder, 16 liter straight petrol engine, which generated 105 horsepower. The tank's armament was two 6-pounder light guns for the male, plus three .303 Hotchkiss machine guns, while the female version carried four .303 Vickers machine guns instead of artillery and a .303 Hotchkiss machine gun. The Mark I-IV, of which over 2,000 models were produced for wartime action, saw service at the Somme, Fleurs-Corciette and Amiens on the Western Front, and during both battles of Gaza in North Africa against Turkish forces.

The British tanks suffered from a number of issues, not least of which was the development of armor-piercing bullets by the Germans in the latter part of the war, and due to mechanical failure or enemy action, only a third of them usually reached enemy positions. However, those that did reach that far almost always contributed significantly to a final victory. A thousand were ordered for later British use, but the end of the conflict brought wartime production to a standstill.

France's initial forays into tank design were not an unqualified success. Unlike the concerted efforts made by the British Armed Forces and the various private companies involved in production, the French initially operated at cross-purposes, thus producing a number of ill-starred early efforts which suffered from some serious design flaws. By 1917, however, thanks primarily to the efforts made by Renault to come up with a successful design, the French were able to field significant numbers of small, agile, and lightly armored tanks. The French envisioned having these tanks operate as a "swarm", a tactic unlike the British but one that was adopted by the Americans, who also purchased and manned the Renault FT. Crewed by just two men, the Renault FT was a little over 15 feet long and weighed just over 6 tons (a third of the Mark I-IVs). It had an operational range of around 40 miles thanks to its 4.5 liter, 4-cylinder Renault petrol engine. The Renault FT was significantly faster than the British tanks, allowing it to operate with a tactical agility reminiscent of what the previous century's cavalry had been able to achieve, and it was also mechanically more reliable. It was far less heavily armed, however, as its two variants being either one single light gun or a single .303 machine gun. Designed to be an agile, fast-hitting screen for maneuverable warfare, over 3000 were produced for use by the French and Americans.

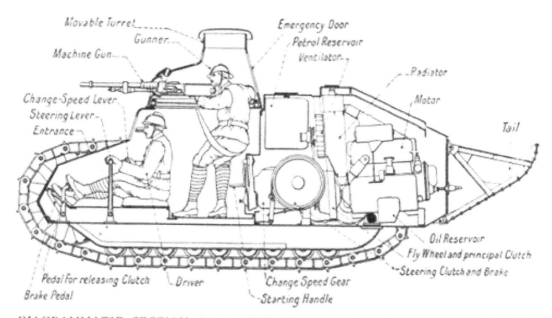

DIAGRAMMATIC SECTION OF A FRENCH LIGHT (OR "MOSQUITO") TANK.

Renault FT "Mosquito" Light Tank

Unlike the remarkable advances the Germans made developing zeppelins, aircraft, heavy artillery and machine guns, they were reluctant to develop tanks and never considered doing so until they found themselves on the receiving end of tank assaults at the Somme. The final product of their efforts was the A7V, envisioned more as an armored troop transport than as an offensive vehicle. Only 20 were eventually produced for battlefield service, but the Germans also employed captured Allied tanks. They saw action on the Western Front at Villers-Bretonneux, where they faced off Against allied tanks in the first tank-on-tank battle, and in other engagements, including the Battles of Aisne and the Marne.

The A7V

The A7V was over 20 feet long and weighed 33 tons, more than even the heaviest Mark I-IVs. It also carried a relatively heavy 57mm gun and six machine guns, and it was powered by two engines: Daimler-Benz 4-cylinders capable of 100 horsepower apiece. This gave it an operational range of between 20-50 miles depending on terrain and fuel tank size, and a top speed of 9 miles per hour on road and 4 miles per hour cross-country. The A7V carried a full complement of 18 men, and in many ways it was a superior machine to its equivalent, the British Mark I-IV, since it was capable of slightly greater speeds and more heavily armed. However, German reluctance to use tanks as a viable battlefield advantage meant that the Germans were never able to field anywhere near the number of vehicles the Allies were.

On September 15, 1916, the first British tank saw action at the Battle of Flers-Courcelette as part of the Somme campaign. The objective was a pair of villages that gave the battle its name. A D1 tank commanded by Captain H. W. Mortimore moved forward, becoming the first tank to see action. Three tanks were supposed to be in the assault on that part of the line, but the other two were delayed.

This was typical all along the line. Initially, 49 tanks were supposed to go into action that morning, but only 32 were ready at zero hour. Five got stuck in trenches or shell craters, nine broke down, and nine moved too slowly to keep up. To their dismay, the crews found that some of the tanks were not fully bulletproof. Bullets hitting the vision slits broke the thick glass, sending slivers into the crewmen's eyes. Bullets hitting the metal sometimes sent spall flying around the interior of the cabin and even punched through the metal plate in the female tanks. The steering tail was found to be pretty much useless when several broke off in the field and the crew realized the tanks maneuvered just as well without them.

Nevertheless, those few tanks that actually made up the vanguard of the attack threw the Germans into a panic, and many men fled at the sight of these lumbering metal beasts. While the attack was only a modest success, the tanks gained the confidence of Haig, who immediately sent an order for 1,000 more.

Four Mark I tanks on the battlefield in September

Mark I vehicles saw regular use in the British sectors, but it was a piecemeal affair in which demand far exceeded supply. They proved their worth in numerous small engagements by taking limited objectives, and the British infantry gained confidence whenever they heard the machines were to join the troops in an assault.

The tank crews also proved their heroism. On November 13, a female tank commanded by Lt. H.W. Hitchcock got stuck in a shell hole. Taking fire, Hitchcock and two of his men were wounded, and the Germans surrounded the tank, firing at it from all sides. Corporal Taffs took over, managed to get the tank free, and continued on to the German second line, where the tank promptly fell through the roof of a German dugout. It was now properly stuck, and at such an angle that it couldn't fire. Once again, the Germans surrounded it and poured machine gun and grenade fire at the helpless tank. Taffs sent out a carrier pigeon with a message calling for help, and about an hour later, the British infantry came to its rescue. All surviving members of the crew earned military medals for their valor.

Ironically, even these accomplishments were somewhat controversial. The French had repeatedly asked the British not to use their tanks before the French ones were ready, preferring to use the British and French tanks in tandem to maximize shock value. It was a sentiment with which many British commanders agreed. In his memoirs, Prime Minister Lloyd George complained that the tanks' "great secret was sold for a battered ruin of a little hamlet on the Somme not worth capturing."

The French feared that the game was up and that the Germans would put smaller field guns on the front line to take out Allied tanks and widen trenches to prevent the tanks from crossing. The Battle of the Somme also led the Schneider Company to modify the design of their tank. Fearing German field guns and the more powerful armor-piercing machine gun rounds the Germans had deployed, the company supplemented the 11.5 mm (.45") armor with a front plate of 8 mm (.31"), placed 20-40 mm in front of the regular armor to reduce the impact from any hits.

The Final Phase of the Battle

The Battle of Flers-Courcelette marked the final phase of the deadly campaign, and though that operation did not achieve its objective of capturing the town of Morval, the Allies gained about 3,000 yards and inflicted considerable casualties. From September 25-28, the Allies took the towns of Combles, Morval, Lesboeufs, and Gueudecourt, and at the Battle of Thiepval Ridge from September 26-28, the British coordinated machine guns, tanks, gas attacks, and infantry together for the first time.

At the start of October, however, operations began to get bogged down in mud and rain, making infantry movement difficult. The wet terrain also dulled the effect of artillery shells. Though nobody knew it at the time, the Battle of the Ancre, fought from November 13-18, was the last major part of the conflict. Haig was able to secure the positions he wanted and prepared for the next assault on enemy positions, but snow covered the ground after the 18th.

By the time the fighting ended, General Haig understood that the war had become one of attrition and put together his battle plans with that in mind. It would have helped to make that realization earlier, because the Allied forces lost many more men than the enemy at the Somme. One detailed estimate puts the Allied casualties at 618,257 and the German casualties at 434,500, which would mean the Allied casualties were about 150% higher than the German casualties.31

However, a war of attrition has to take into account more than soldiers. The war involved tons of equipment, and morale and exhaustion all played roles. Historians now believe that the Germans lost many important officers who could not be replaced, and one German general, Generalleutnant Von Fuchs, said in January 1917, "Enemy superiority is so great that we are not in a position either to fix their forces in position or to prevent them from launching an offensive elsewhere. We just do not have the troops.... We cannot prevail in a second battle of the Somme with our men; they cannot achieve that any more."32

Both sides seemed aware that the Germans were exhausted. British guns reached well beyond the first line of trenches so that German soldiers far back behind the lines never got any rest, and if the war was a material war as the Germans claimed, the British were winning at the Somme. Every month, they brought in more supplies, to the point that five months into the campaign, they were bringing in twice the tonnage. The Germans were probably aware of this thanks to aerial reconnaissance, which could not have helped morale.33

Two months after the start of the Battle of the Somme, the German High Command went through a shakeup. General von Falkenhayn was replaced by General von Hindenburg, a replacement that due to a number of factors, the Battle of the Somme being chief among them. It was no accident that after 1916, the Germans decided to build a new defensive position known as the Hindenburg Line. In Germany, it was known as the Siegfriedstellung (the Siegfried Line), after the famous mythological hero who was a central figure in Wagner's operas.

Although the Germans began construction of the Siegfried Line in September 1916, it was still under construction when they retired to that position in March 1917, so they did not have the advantage they had at the Somme of carefully constructing their defenses over a long period of time.

The Legacy of the Battle

While it could hardly be said anybody won the Battle of the Somme, the battle of attrition served the Allies well, especially when the Americans joined the war in 1918.

From March 21-July 18, 1918, the German armies launched their last great offensive – the *Kaiserschlacht*. The "Kaiser's Battle" consisted of four main offensives launched all along the northern portion of the Western Front: Operations Michael, Georgette, Gneisenau and Blucher-

---

31 Wendt, H. L. *Verdun 1916 The attacks by Falkenhayn in the Meuse area towards Verdun as a strategic question.* Berlin, 1931, Mittler. OCLC 503838028, p. 246.

32 Sheldon, J. *The German Army at Cambrai.* Barnsley, 2009, Pen & Sword Books, p. 4.

33 Henniker, A. M.. *Transportation on the Western Front 1914–1918.* History of the Great War Based on Official Documents by Direction of the Historical Section of the Committee of Imperial Defence (Imperial War Museum and Battery Press ed.). London: HMSO, (2009) [1937], p. 179.

Yorck. The objective of the *Kaiserschlacht* was simple: all-out victory or ruinous defeat, death or glory. There was no other alternative. The stalemate of the Western Front had sapped Germany and Austria's resources, while in the Mediterranean their ally Turkey was suffering against ANZAC and Imperial troops. While the collapse of Russia as a nation had freed dozens of divisions from the icy bloodbath of the Eastern Front, these troops were battle-weary and lacking equipment, hardly crack reinforcements.

The Allies themselves were hardly in better shape, the French army in particular having been all but bled dry, although Italy and even Portugal were providing some much needed reinforcements. However, there was one key factor which had the German High Command seriously worried, and led to the all-or-nothing assault on the Western front: the entry of the United States into the war. Although the initial commitment of the US was a small Expeditionary Force, equipped primarily with French vehicles and armor, these were high-caliber reinforcements – fresh and eager with previous campaign experience. Above all, Germany knew that once America was well and truly committed, its overwhelming superiority in industrial output (untouched thus far by war) and potential troop numbers would dwarf any other army currently in the field. Because of this, the Allies had to be crushed swiftly and decisively, and if this could not be achieved, Germany would lose.

At this point in the war, Germany was still, with millions of men under arms and enough materiel to supply them, a fearsome fighting force; it was not yet the dying but still lethal beast it would be during the Hundred Days Offensive. Yet as powerful as it was, the German Army was feeling the strain. In *All Quiet on the Western Front,* Erich Maria Remarque (who served in World War I himself) paints a harrowing portrait of the state of the army at that time (albeit through the eyes of a semi-fictional set of characters), which sums up better than any other description the state of the *Deutsches Heer.*

> "Our lines are falling back. There are too many fresh English and American regiments over there. There's too much corned beef and white wheaten bread. Too many new guns. Too many aeroplanes.

> But we are emaciated and starved. Our food is bad and mixed up with so much substitute stuff that it makes us ill. The factory owners in Germany have grown wealthy;--dysentery dissolves our bowels […]

> Our artillery is fired out, it has too few shells and the barrels are so worn that they shoot uncertainly, and scatter so widely as even to fall on ourselves. We have too few horses. Our fresh troops are anaemic boys in need of rest, who cannot carry a pack, but merely know how to die. By thousands. They understand nothing about warfare, they simply go on and let themselves be shot down. A single flyer routed two companies of them for a joke, just as they came fresh from the train--before they had ever heard of such a thing as cover.

'Germany ought to be empty soon,' says Kat."

Despite their forces being stretched perilously thin, on March 21st, 1918 the German Army launched a full-scale assault, the brainchild of General Erich Ludendorff (after whom the offensive is sometimes named). The main assault, Operation Michael, was launched in the Somme area against the (primarily) British and French troops stationed there, with the other assaults being corollary attacks designed to pin down any reinforcements which might otherwise have been funneled into the Somme battleground to halt the German advance. The broad outline of Ludendorff's scheme was in a similar vein to the original intent of the Schlieffen Plan; the intention was to break through the center of the Allied defenses and split them apart, shattering the defensive line and, ideally, driving all the way to the sea in order to sever the lines of supply and reinforcement which made them so stolid and impregnable. The British Army would be outflanked, encircled, and starved or battered into submission, at which point, Ludendorff believed, the French would surrender.

Initially, Michael was a remarkable success. Following the most extensive and prolonged barrage of the war, German stormtroopers assaulted British and French positions, travelling across No Man's Land with lightning speed and storming the enemy trenches before the defenders had a chance to take their place on the firesteps and man the machine gun positions after the barrage. In terms of territorial gains, the Spring Offensive was actually one of the most successful in the entire war up to that point, second only to the initial German assault in 1914. During the course of the entire offensive, the Allies lost over 800,000 men (most of them French and British) killed, captured or wounded, and in Operation Michael alone, the Germans took or destroyed 1300 artillery pieces and 200 tanks.

Ultimately, however, the *Kaiserschlacht* was a disaster for the Germans. The Allied line bent but did not break, and the German offensives were held up everywhere, unable to secure the vital breakthrough which would have enabled Ludendorff's plan to achieve strategic success. The Germans themselves lost almost 700,000 men, and their well of manpower was far shallower at this point than the Allies', particularly with the Americans yet to seriously commit to the war. Crucially, the 700,000 dead were almost all from the elite German *stosstruppen* regiments, highly trained, fit, veteran infantrymen who were at this point irreplaceable given the dwindling source of German wartime manpower. Additionally, the very success of the operation was part of its downfall; the German stormtroopers could cover rough ground at speed, but the same was not true for their supply lines and reinforcements, who struggled to forge ahead through the shell-blasted territory of no man's land and the wreckage of what had been the Franco-British lines. The main forward element of the German Army found itself occupying a vulnerable salient that could be assaulted from three sides, short of ammunition, food and medical supplies, and essentially cut off from the main force of the advance.

The *Kaiserschlacht* had been the last gasp of a dying giant; it had given the Allies a serious scare, but they had weathered the storm and could now retaliate with the hammer blow which would break the German resistance once and for all, thereby bringing about the fabled "end to all wars". All that was needed was the plan, men, materiel, and will to decisively defeat the Germans.

The end finally came in November 1918. At 11:00 a.m. on the 11th day of the 11th month, the "war to end all wars" finally came to an end. The Armistice brought about the cessation of all offensive activities in Europe, and the points detailed in the text of the armistice itself were mainly decided by Marshal Foch. Though based upon Woodrow Wilson's Fourteen Points, what they meant in brief was a complete and utter defeat for Germany. All military hostilities were to cease immediately within six hours, and Germany would withdraw all remaining troops from France, Luxembourg, Belgium and Alsace-Lorraine within two weeks. The Germans would also be obliged to pull back from their positions in Turkey, Romania and Austro-Hungary and resume the 1914 border line. Likewise, they would have to withdraw all forces on the Western front to the Rhine and submit to Allied occupation of a buffer zone. The German navy would also be confined to port, and all its submarines surrendered to the Allies, along with 5,000 artillery pieces, 25,000 machine guns, 3,000 mortars, 1,700 airplanes, 5,000 train locomotives and 150,000 train cars.

Only after the war could the legacy of the Battle of the Somme be objectively considered, and it is still the subject of great debate. Haig is still one of the most controversial military figures in British history, and people continue to debate whether he was the "Butcher of the Somme"[34] (as he was nicknamed after his death) or "the man who won the war" as the American General John J. Pershing said of him.[35]

Even Winston Churchill and Lloyd George had mixed opinions. Churchill said that Haig's actions at the Somme unnecessarily weakened the British army by using tactics that did not take into account the new realities of war. Furthermore, given that World War I was a battle of attrition, the fact that the Germans lost less than the British would suggest they got the better of it. Nevertheless, Churchill believed Haig vindicated himself at the end of the war by breaking through the German Hindenburg Line and capturing almost 200,000 German soldiers. Lloyd George, after having been Prime Minister, was much more critical but at the same time described Haig as brilliant.

It seems clear that Haig was the most qualified man to lead the British Army, and, like most commanders, he made the mistake of "fighting the last war." Having said that, it's only fair to admit that he had serious flaws and blind spots, and these flaws cost the lives of perhaps tens of

---

34 Walsh, Ben. "The Plan" ("The Somme > Background"). The National Archives, www.nationalarchives.gov.uk/education/greatwar/g4/cs3/background.htm. Accessed March 8, 2019.
35 Corrigan, Gordon. *Mud, Blood & Poppycock.* Cassell, 2002, p. 204.

thousands of young soldiers.

For example, he did not have a flexible command structure.36 The battle was pre-planned from the beginning and there was virtually no way for soldiers and officers to adjust to the conditions that they encountered. Thus, rather than running the battle from their headquarters, the commanders ended up being spectators who found out, long after a particular skirmish was over, what had occurred. Put simply, the British weren't properly dealing with the fog of war, as illustrated by the memo Haig sent out toward the end of the first day of the Battle of the Somme: "North of the Ancre, VIII Division (sic) said they began well but as the day progressed, their troops were forced back into the German front line, except two battalions which occupied Serre Village and were, it is said, cut off. I am inclined to believe from further reports that few of VIII Corps left their trenches."37

A faulty command structure, an inflexible response, and a poor communication system led to the needless deaths of nearly 20,000 men, but Haig shrugged off the terrible losses on the first day of the Battle of the Somme and ordered that the fighting continue the next day and then for months after, which also caused heavy losses. Ironically, he criticized the Germans for doing exactly the same thing, writing, "In spite of throwing already 106 Divisions into the battle and enduring the most reckless sacrifice of human life, [the German Military] has as yet made little progress towards his goals."38

It is quite likely that Haig saw his troops as numbers instead of people. On the battlefield that made sense, but when the news came back to Britain that an entire generation of young men from a village had been wiped out, it affected the public quite a bit differently.

Like generals on both sides of the conflict, Haig was accused of being aloof and an aristocratic individual who did not really understand the needs of the common man and the workers who made up most of his army. Haig was known to have preferred gentlemen as aides and subordinates, but at this point in history, the officers were aristocrats and the fighting men were lower class. This was one of the reasons that so many men felt betrayed after the war, as the burden had fallen on the most vulnerable.

However, to be fair to Haig, he felt from the beginning that his troops were not ready to fight. He only did so because the French insisted the start of the battle be moved up to take the pressure off the German offensive at Verdun. Add into the mix the fact that he preferred another location for a battle, and it's clear that Haig faced a difficult situation at the start of July 1916.

---

36 Travers, Tim. *How the War Was Won*. Routledge, 1992, pp. 54, 66–70.

37 Sheffield, G.; Bourne, J., eds. *Douglas Haig: War Diaries and Letters 1914–1918* (BCA ed.). London: Weidenfeld & and Nicolson, 2005, p. 196.

38 Doyle, Arthur Conan. *The British Campaign in France and Flanders, Volume 5*. London, Hodder and Stoughton, 1919, p. 148.

As for the soldiers who survived World War I, it was often said that they were "destroyed by war, even though they might have escaped its shells."39 Before the Great War, there seemed to be a mystique and glory that encompassed the notion of war in Europe. After all, the war was being fought just a few generations removed from Napoleon.

As an industrial war, World War I was different, but few men talked about their experiences. Today, it is well understood that many suffered from PTSD and survivor's guilt, so even those who were not severely injured had been changed. They knew that they had experienced something that they hoped would never reoccur, and they wanted to protect their families and children from this reality. According to sources, "Of the 60 million soldiers who fought in the First World War, over 9 million were killed — 14% of the combat troops or 6,000 dead soldiers per day. The armies of the Central Powers mobilized 25 million soldiers and 3.5 million of them died. The Entente Powers deployed 40 million soldiers and lost more than 5 million." About 21 million soldiers were wounded altogether.40 It's hardly a wonder then that so many Europeans bent over backwards to avoid another war in the 1930s.

According to Ernest Hemingway, Gertrude Stein heard an angry French garage owner admonish his young veteran employee with the words "génération perdue," calling him part of a lost generation. She later repeated this phrase to Hemingway and the American expatriates, telling them, "You are all a lost generation." Hemingway used this term in his novel, *The Sun Also Rises*, and it became a popular label for the veterans.

After a while, "Lost Generation" took on many different meanings. It referred to young soldiers who had been in the war, but who no longer felt a part of their society when they came back home. It referred to soldiers who felt betrayed by their country, their teachers, and their officers. It meant that they no longer had the same moral compass they had before the war and did not know how to replace it. It meant that they did not know how to put their lives back together once the war was over. It meant that the memory of war, horrible as it was, had more reality and truth than working life during peacetime.

Perhaps the best description came from a German soldier who served at the front, Erich Maria Remarque. He wrote the anti-war novel *All Quiet on the Western Front*, which was later made into a famous movie. Remarque wrote:

> "There were thousands of Kantoreks [the name of his teacher who convinced his
> students to sign up], all of whom were convinced that they were acting for the best--

---

39 Remarque, Erich Maria. *All Quiet on the Western Front.* Translated from the German by A. W. Wheen Fawcett Crest. New York, Random House Trade Paperbacks; Reissue edition (September 29, 1996), p. 1.

40 Royde-Smith, John Graham & The Editors of Encyclopaedia Britannica. "Killed, Wounded, And Missing." Encyclopaedia Britannica, https://www.britannica.com/event/World-War-I/Killed-wounded-and-missing. Accessed March 8, 2019.

in a way that cost them nothing. And that is why they let us down so badly. For us lads of eighteen they ought to have been mediators and guides to the world of maturity, the world of work, of duty, of culture, of progress--to the future. We often made fun of them and played jokes on them, but in our hearts we trusted them. The idea of authority, which they represented, was associated in our minds with a greater insight and a more humane wisdom. But the first death we saw shattered this belief. We had to recognize that our generation was more to be trusted than theirs. They surpassed us only in phrases and in cleverness. The first bombardment showed us our mistake, and under it the world as they had taught it to us broke in pieces.41

"Now if we go back, we will be weary, broken, burnt out, rootless, and without hope. We will not be able to find our way any more. And men will not understand us--for the generation that grew up before us, though it has passed these years with us already had a home and a calling; now it will return to its old occupations, and the war will be forgotten--and the generation that has grown up after us will be strange to us and push us aside. We will be superfluous even to ourselves, we will grow older, a few will adapt themselves, some others will merely submit, and most will be bewildered;--the years will pass by and in the end we shall fall into ruin."42

Soldiers' Poetry from the Somme

*I HAVE A RENDEZVOUS WITH DEATH*43

By Alan Seeger

I have a rendezvous with Death

At some disputed barricade,

When Spring comes back with rustling shade

And apple-blossoms fill the air –

I have a rendezvous with Death

When Spring brings back blue days and fair.

---

41 Remarque, p 11.
42 Ibid., p. 214.
43 Walter, George (editor). *The Penguin Book of First World War Poetry.* Penguin Classics; 1 edition (May 11, 2007). Reprinted in the section: Poets of the Somme, https://www.penguin.co.uk/articles/2016/poets-of-the-somme/. Accessed March 8, 2019.

It may be he shall take my hand

And lead me into his dark land

And close my eyes and quench my breath –

It may be I shall pass him still.

I have a rendezvous with Death

On some scarred slope of battered hill,

When Spring comes round again this year

And the first meadow-flowers appear.

God knows 'twere better to be deep

Pillowed in silk and scented down,

Where Love throbs out in blissful sleep,

Pulse nigh to pulse, and breath to breath,

Where hushed awakenings are dear . . .

But I've a rendezvous with Death

At midnight in some flaming town,

When Spring trips north again this year,

And I to my pledged word am true,

I shall not fail that rendezvous.

Alan Seeger died on July 4, 1916, at the Battle of the Somme.

DULCE ET DECORUM EST[44]

By Wilfred Owen

---

[44] Owen Wilfred. *Poems By Wilfred Owen*. London: Chatto and Windus, 1921.

Bent double, like old beggars under sacks,

Knock-kneed, coughing like hags, we cursed through sludge,

Till on the haunting flares we turned our backs,

And towards our distant rest began to trudge.

Men marched asleep. Many had lost their boots,

But limped on, blood-shod. All went lame; all blind;

Drunk with fatigue; deaf even to the hoots

Of gas-shells dropping softly behind.

Gas! GAS! Quick, boys!—An ecstasy of fumbling

Fitting the clumsy helmets just in time,

But someone still was yelling out and stumbling

And flound'ring like a man in fire or lime.—

Dim through the misty panes and thick green light,

As under a green sea, I saw him drowning.

In all my dreams before my helpless sight,

He plunges at me, guttering, choking, drowning.

If in some smothering dreams, you too could pace

Behind the wagon that we flung him in,

And watch the white eyes writhing in his face,

His hanging face, like a devil's sick of sin;

If you could hear, at every jolt, the blood

Come gargling from the froth-corrupted lungs,

Obscene as cancer, bitter as the cud

Of vile, incurable sores on innocent tongues,—

My friend, you would not tell with such high zest

To children ardent for some desperate glory,

The old Lie: Dulce et decorum est

Pro patria mori. [Latin for "it is sweet and fitting to die for one's country."]

Wilfred Owen was killed in battle a week before the armistice was signed in November 1918.

Online Resources

Other World War I titles by Charles River Editors

Other titles about the Somme on Amazon

Bibliography

Begbie, Harold. "Fall In." Lyrics quoted by George Upton in his book *The Song: Its Birth, Evolution, and Functions.* Chicago, A.C. McClurg & Co., 1915.

Badsey, S. (1983). "Battle of the Somme: British War-Propaganda." Historical Journal of Film, Radio and Television. 3 (2): 99 doi:10.1080/01439688300260081. ISSN 0143-9685.

Baker, Chris. "British artillery bombardment before the infantry attack on the Somme." THE LONG, LONG TRAIL, 2019, www.longlongtrail.co.uk/battles/battles-of-the-western-front-in-france-and-flanders/the-battles-of-the-somme-1916/british-artillery-bombardment-before-the-infantry-attack-on-the-somme/. Accessed March 8, 2019.

The Battle of the Somme (1916 film), Official War Film, distributed by British Topical Committee for War Films. Available at: https://www.youtube.com/watch?v=xQ_OZfaiUlc. Accessed March 8, 2019.

Brown, G.I. *The Big Bang: a History of Explosives.* Sutton Publishing, 1998.

Comments in the Great War Forum. "Taking no prisoners." https://www.greatwarforum.org/topic/78568-taking-no-prisoners/. Accessed March 8, 2019.

Coppard, George. Quote from a machine gunner at the Battle of the Somme. Reprinted by

Trueman, C. N. "The Battle Of The Somme." The History Learning Site, Apr 2015, www.historylearningsite.co.uk/world-war-one/battles-of-world-war-one/the-battle-of-the-somme/17. Accessed March 8, 2019.

Corrigan, Gordon. *Mud, Blood & Poppycock.* Cassell, 2002.

Daniels, Patricia."History of Trench Warfare in World War I." ThoughtCo, August 13, 2018, www.thoughtco.com/trenches-in-world-war-i-1779981. Accessed March 8, 2019.

Doyle, Arthur Conan. *The British Campaign in France and Flanders, Volume 5.* London, Hodder and Stoughton, 1919.

Duffy, Michael. "Weapons of War - Machine Guns" ("British Army Rejection"). firstworldwar, 22 August, 2009, www.firstworldwar.com/weaponry/machineguns.htm. Accessed March 8, 2019.

Eliot, T. S. *Selected Poems.* Houghton Mifflin Harcourt, 2014.

Foley, R. T. *German Strategy and the Path to Verdun: Erich von Falkenhayn and the Development of Attrition, 1870–1916* (pbk. ed.). Cambridge: CUP., 2007.

GCSE section for UK teachers. http://www.markedbyteachers.com/gcse/history/douglas-haig-butcher-or-hero.html. Accessed March 8, 2019.

Gibbs, Philip. Journalist quoted in *Reporting from the Front: War Reporters During the Great War* by Brian Best. Pen and Sword, Nov 30, 2014.

Haig, General Douglas, (D. HAIG, General, Commanding-in-Chief, British Armies in France). "Sir Douglas Haig's 2nd Despatch (Somme), 23 December 1916." https://www.firstworldwar.com/source/haigsommedespatch.htm. Accessed March 8, 2019.

Henniker, A. M.. *Transportation on the Western Front 1914–1918.* History of the Great War Based on Official Documents by Direction of the Historical Section of the Committee of Imperial Defence (Imperial War Museum and Battery Press ed.). London: HMSO, (2009) [1937].

Hogg, Ian and Batchelor, John. *Weapons & War Machines.* New York, Crescent Books, 1975.

Howse, Christopher. "Shrines built while the First World War went on." THE TELEGRAPH, Jun 2009, www.telegraph.co.uk/comment/columnists/christopherhowse/5581520/Shrines-built-while-the-First-World-War-went-on.html. Accessed March 8, 2019.

Irvine, John. Report in the "Daily Express" on July 3rd 1916. Reprinted by Jones, Simon. *Underground Warfare 1914-1918.* Barnsley: Pen & Sword Books, 2010.

Lewis, Jon E. A *Brief History of the First World War: Eyewitness Accounts of the War to End All Wars. 1914–18*, Hachette UK, 2014.

"Pals Battalions" ("BATTLE OF THE SOMME"). Yorkshire Reporter, November 7, 2016, www.yorkshirereporter.co.uk/zyxc/battle-of-the-somme/. Accessed March 8, 2019.

Rees, Nigel. *Brewer's Famous Quotations*. Weidenfeld & Nicolson, 2006.

Remarque, Erich Maria. *All Quiet on the Western Front*. Translated from the German by A. W. Wheen. New York, Random House Trade Paperbacks; Reissue edition (September 29, 1996).

Royde-Smith, John Graham & The Editors of Encyclopaedia Britannica. "Killed, Wounded, And Missing." Encyclopaedia Britannica, https://www.britannica.com/event/World-War-I/Killed-wounded-and-missing. Accessed March 8, 2019.

Sheffield, G.; Bourne, J., eds. *Douglas Haig: War Diaries and Letters 1914–1918* (BCA ed.). London: Weidenfeld & and Nicolson, 2005.

Sheldon, J. (2009). *The German Army at Cambrai*. Barnsley, 2009, Pen & Sword Books.

Travers, Tim. *How the War Was Won*. Routledge, 1992.

von Richthofen, Captain Manfred Freiherr. *The Red Battle Flyer*. Translated by Ellis Barker, M. Dent & Sons, Ltd. Toronto, Canada 1918.

Walsh, Ben. "The Plan" ("The Somme > Background"). The National Archives, www.nationalarchives.gov.uk/education/greatwar/g4/cs3/background.htm. Accessed March 8, 2019.

Walter, George (editor). *The Penguin Book of First World War Poetry*. Penguin Classics; 1 edition (May 11, 2007). Reprinted in the section: "Poets of the Somme," https://www.penguin.co.uk/articles/2016/poets-of-the-somme/. Accessed March 8, 2019.

"War's Realities on the Cinema". The Times. London. 22 August 1916. ISSN 0140-0460.

Wendt, H. L. *Verdun 1916 The attacks by Falkenhayn in the Meuse area towards Verdun as a strategic question*. Berlin, 1931, Mittler. OCLC 503838028.

Whitehead, R. J. (2013). *The Other Side of the Wire: The Battle of the Somme. With the German XIV Reserve Corps, 1 July 1916. II. Solihull: Helion*.

Zuber, T. *The Real German War Plan 1904–14* (e-book ed.). New York: The History Press, 2010.

Zuckerman, Larry. *The Rape of Belgium: The Untold Story of World War I.* New York University Press, 2004.

Wylly, Colonel H.C. *Crown and Company. The Historical Records of the 2nd Battalion Royal Dublin Fusiliers, Volume II, 1911-1922.* Aldershot, 1923.

Free Books by Charles River Editors

We have brand new titles available for free most days of the week. To see which of our titles are currently free, click on this link.

Discounted Books by Charles River Editors

We have titles at a discount price of just 99 cents everyday. To see which of our titles are currently 99 cents, click on this link.

Made in the USA
Las Vegas, NV
09 October 2024

96578764R00044